DEVELOPING

EFFICIENT READING

DEPARTMENT OF EDUCATION
PROVIDENCE COLLEGE
PROVIDENCE 8, RHODE ISLAND

DEVELOPING

EFFICIENT READING

LEONARD S. BRAAM
School of Education, Syracuse University
AND
WILLIAM D. SHELDON
School of Education, Syracuse University

New York
OXFORD UNIVERSITY PRESS
1959

PRINTED IN THE UNITED STATES OF AMERICA

Contents

Introduction

THIS BOOK was prepared to meet the need for a new program for reading improvement at the college level. This program stresses the development of a flexible approach to reading. The text includes pre-tests and post-tests of reading flexibility. It relates reading instruction to courses being taken. When students complete a reading improvement course using these materials, it is hoped that they will have gained a more flexible and useful approach to reading, increased their vocabulary, and improved their ability to study through more efficient reading.

The Need for Reading Courses in College

A NUMBER of successful college reading programs have been reported. One program developed at Northwestern University reported the problems and progress in reading of ninety college students. The gains made during a single quarter were very gratifying. According to the report, the average grade scores of freshmen on the Iowa Silent Reading Test increased from the 28th to the 52nd percentile for college norms. The average scores of upper-class students improved from the 48th to the 76th percentile. In addition, the average rate of reading for the students increased from 272 words to 474 words a minute, with a marked improvement in comprehension.

In a reading program held at Western Michigan College, improvement in reading was noted for some sixty-two students. One of the authors reports a successful program at Syracuse University with medical students. During one semester's instruction in reading, each student improved in both his over-all reading ability and in his rate of comprehension. A further review of the literature reveals hundreds of examples of similar programs which have helped college students to read and study with more success.

Parents, taxpayers, and many college professors have raised the question: "Why should we need to teach reading at the college level?" "Why wasn't reading mastered before students reach the college level?"

Psychologists and educators who have studied the reading process come up with rather simple reasons concerning the need for teaching reading at the college level. Some of these reasons, based on research, are:

1. Reading is a developmental process which is never completely mastered. Improvement can be made in using reading as a process for learning all through life. There is evidence that children, adolescents, young adults, and mature individuals can improve their mastery over the process of reading.

2. Because of an expanding demand for reading, new approaches to the increase of reading efficiency are needed. The simple and direct material used in the elementary school, with its scope limited by the needs and experiences of the young readers, presents a far different task for mastery than the complex material used at the college level. For example, an assignment in the elementary school may well be set by the reading of several straightforward, factual paragraphs in a single textbook. On the other hand, an assignment in a college history or science course might require the skimming of many source materials, the rapid reading of other sources, and the more careful study of a few, in order to obtain the answers required and the integration of materials from varied sources.

3. Reading is also a process that demands continuous and specific practice in order that efficiency be maintained at a high level. The college reading course provides for such practice in a limited fashion and, more important, gives the student an insight into what needs to be done to maintain efficiency.

Reading has been taught to students at Syracuse University since 1925. The present program received a great impetus due to the thousands of returned veterans who flooded the campus in the years following the Second World War. Today the program continues to serve 20 to 30 per cent of the freshmen entering the University.

A survey of the thousands of freshmen taught at Syracuse University indicates that freshmen have the following major weaknesses in reading:

1. Lack of flexibility.
2. Poor comprehension of general and specific details.
3. Lack of confidence in their ability to read.

It is the belief of the authors, based on their experience with thousands of college students, that reading can be improved and that this improved reading can affect in a positive manner the academic progress of the students concerned.

How To Use the Book

Developing Efficient Reading is designed to be used either by students in a group classroom situation under the supervision and guidance of an instructor, or by the student who wishes to develop and improve his reading and study skills individually and independently.

An inspection of the table of contents will reveal that the philosophy of "test—teach (or learn)—test" is employed. Section I provides pre-tests of Flexibility in Reading, Vocabulary, and a Study Skills Check List. The tests and check list are designed to help each student assess his own level of functioning in each of these areas.

Sections II, III, and IV provide for the development of increased efficiency in reading.

Section V provides a second series of tests which permit the student to evaluate his improved competency in these areas.

It is recommended that the book be used in the sequence in which it is presented. All the pre-test materials should be covered before starting work on any of the exercises in sections II, III, or IV. These pre-test materials should be covered in as few sessions as possible.

It is recommended that a schedule of frequent, relatively short periods of time be established for doing the exercises provided in sections II, III, and IV. Setting aside a short period (20 to 30 minutes) per day to attack the problem of improving reading efficiency is most desirable. Such a schedule will produce much better results than devoting a full evening or half a day once a week to the improvement of reading skills.

After completing the exercises in sections II, III, and IV, it is recommended that the post-tests in section V be completed. A comparison of the results of your achievement on exercises in sections I and V will then provide a picture of the improvement made in these skills.

I—Pre-Tests

FLEXIBILITY OF READING PRE-TEST

How Flexible Is Your Reading?

Do YOU know how flexible you are in your approach to reading of different kinds of materials? Do you know how rapidly you read? Do you know how well you understand or recall what you read? If you are not sure, the following test gives you an opportunity to diagnose your own reading.

The object of the following test is to find out at what rate per minute you can read various kinds of material with good understanding. The following selections cover five different subjects and are of varying levels of difficulty and of familiarity. Read the selections and time yourself on each one. Place your time in the proper box below each selection. Answer the questions and then go on to the next selection. When you have finished all five selections go back and compute your rate per minute and your percentage of comprehension for each selection.

NARRATIVE PRE-TEST

Purpose: To read as quickly as you can and still understand the general content of this selection.

Procedure: Record the time (hour, minutes, seconds) when you begin reading the selection. After reading the selection, again record the time. Then answer the questions related to the selection.

Beginning Time:

Hour: _____ Minutes: _____ Seconds: _____

(900 words)

Rest Stop for the Sanderlings

THE NIGHT when the great run of shad was passing through the inlet and into the river estuary was a night, too, of vast movements of birds into the sound country.

At daybreak and at half tide two small sanderlings ran beside the dark water on the ocean beach of the barrier island, keeping in the thin film at the edge of the ebbing surf. They were trim little birds in rust and gray plumage, and they ran with a twinkle of black feet over the hard-packed sand, where puffs of blown spume or sea froth rolled like thistledown. They belonged to a flock of several hundred shore birds that had arrived from the south during the night. The migrants had rested in the lee of the great dunes while darkness remained; now growing light and ebbing water were drawing them to the sea's edge.

As the two sanderlings probed the wet sand for small, thin-shelled crustaceans, they forgot the long flight of the night before in the excitement of the hunt. For the moment they forgot, too, that faraway place which they must reach before many days had passed—a place of vast tundras, of snow-fed lakes, and midnight sun. Blackfoot, leader of the migrant flock, was making his fourth journey from the southernmost tip of South America to the Arctic nesting grounds of his kind. In his short lifetime he had traveled more than sixty thousand miles, following the sun north and south across the globe, some eight thousand miles spring and fall. The little hen sanderling that ran beside him on the beach was a yearling, returning for the first time to the Arctic she had left as a fledgling nine months before. Like the older sanderlings, Silverbar had changed her winter plumage of pearly gray for a mantle heavily splashed with cinnamon and rust, the colors worn by all sanderlings on their return to their first home.

In the fringe of the surf, Blackfoot and Silverbar sought the sand bugs or Hippa crabs that honeycombed the ocean beach with their burrowings. Of all the food of the tide zone they loved best these small, egg-shaped crabs. After the retreat of each wave the wet sand bubbled with the air released from the shallow crab burrows, and a sanderling could, if he were quick and sure of foot, insert his bill and draw out the crab before the next wave came tumbling in. Many of the crabs were washed out by the swift rushes of the waves and left kicking in liquefying sand. Often the sanderlings seized these crabs in the moment of their confusion, before they could bury themselves by furious scrambling.

Pressing close to the backwash, Silverbar saw two shining air bubbles pushing away the sand grains and she knew that a crab was beneath. Even as she watched the bubbles her bright eyes saw that a wave was taking form in the tumbling confusion of the surf. She gauged the speed of the mound of water as it ran, toppling, up the beach. Above the deeper undertones of moving water she heard the lighter hiss that came as the crest began to spill. Almost in the same instant the feathered antennae of the crab appeared above the sand. Running under the very crest of the green water hill, Silverbar probed vigorously in the wet sand with opened bill and drew out the crab.

A tern came flying along the surf line,

his black-capped head bent and his eyes alert for the movement of fish in the water. He watched the sanderlings closely, for sometimes a small beach bird could be frightened into giving up its catch. When the tern saw Blackfoot run swiftly into the path of a wave and seize a crab he slanted down menacingly, screaming threats in a shrill, grating voice.

Tee-ar-r-r! Tee-ar-r-r! rattled the tern.

The swoop of the white-winged bird, which was twice as large as the sanderling, took Blackfoot by surprise, for his senses had been occupied with eluding the onrush of water and preventing the escape of the large crab held in his bill. He sprang into the air with a sharp Keet! Keet! and circled out over the surf. The tern whirled after him in pursuit, crying loudly.

In his ability to bank and pivot in the air Blackfoot was fully the equal of the tern. The two birds, darting and twisting and turning, coming up sharply together and falling away again into the wave troughs, passed out beyond the breakers and the sound of their voices was lost to the sanderling flock on the beach.

As he rose steeply into the air in pursuit of Blackfoot, the tern caught sight of a glint of silver in the water below. He bent his head to mark the new prey more certainly and saw the green water spangled with silver streaks as the sun struck the flanks of a school of feeding silversides. Instantly the tern tipped his body steeply into a plane perpendicular to the water. He fell like a stone, although his body could not have weighed more than a few ounces, struck the water with a splash and a shower of spray, and in a matter of seconds emerged with a fish curling in his bill. By this time Blackfoot, forgotten by the tern in the excitement engendered by the bright flashes in the water, had reached the shore and dropped down among the feeding sanderlings, where he was running and probing busily as before.

Ending Time:

Hour: _____ Minutes: _____ Seconds: _____

NARRATIVE I—*Rest Stop for the Sanderlings*

Comprehension Check

Indicate whether, according to the selection just read, each of the following statements is true or false.

1. T F The plumage of the sanderlings was rust and gray.
2. T F The sanderlings were flying from the Arctic to the tip of South America.
3. T F The sanderling was smaller than the tern.
4. T F The tern was distracted from pursuing Blackfoot by the sight of a new winged enemy.
5. T F The tern weighed but a few ounces.
6. T F The sanderlings arrived in the river estuary during a run of shad.
7. T F Sanderlings flew as much as six thousand miles in a season.
8. T F The sanderlings were born in the Arctic.
9. T F Sanderlings are noted for their call, Tee-ar-r-r! Tee-ar-r-r!
10. T F The tern swooped and caught a silverside.

Now check your answers with the key on page 16. Then determine your percentage of comprehension by checking in the table below.

Number of Answers Correct	10	9	8	7	6	5	4	3	2	1
Percentage of Comprehension	100	90	80	70	60	50	40	30	20	10

Reading Rate: In the spaces below fill in the times when you began and finished reading the selection. Subtract the beginning time from the ending time. Now check your rate of reading to the nearest time unit in the table below.

	Hour	Minutes	Seconds
Ending Time:	_____	_____	_____
Beginning Time:	_____	_____	_____
Total Reading Time:	_____	_____	_____

Time	1′00″	1′15″	1′30″	1′45″	2′00″	2′15″	2′30″	2′45″	3′00″
W.P.M.	900	787	675	562	450	412	375	337	300

Time	3′15″	3′30″	3′45″	4′00″	4′15″	4′30″	4′45″	5′00″
W.P.M.	281	262	243	225	213	202	191	180

LITERATURE PRE-TEST

Purpose: To read as quickly as you can and still understand the general content of this selection.

Procedure: Record the time (hour, minutes, seconds) when you begin reading the selection. After reading the selection, again record the time. Then answer the questions related to the selection.

Beginning Time:

Hour: _____ Minutes: _____ Seconds: _____

(742 words)

Cortés Makes an Ally

THE FOLLOWING morning, Cortés, accompanied by fifty of his men, paid a visit to the lord of Cempoalla in his own residence. It was a building of stone and lime, standing on a steep terrace of earth, and was reached by a flight of stone steps. It may have borne resemblance in its structure to some of the ancient buildings found in Central America. Cortés, leaving his soldiers in the courtyard, entered the mansion with one of his officers, and his fair interpreter, Doña Marina. A long conference ensued, from which the Spanish general gathered much light respecting the state of the country. He first announced to the chief, that he was the subject of a great monarch who dwelt beyond the waters; that he had come to the Aztec shores, to abolish the inhuman worship which prevailed there, and to introduce the knowledge of the true God. The cacique replied, that their gods, who sent them the sunshine and the rain, were good enough for them; that he was the tributary of a powerful monarch also, whose capital stood on a lake far off among the mountains; a stern prince, merciless in his exactions, and, in case of resistance, or any

William Prescott. From *The Oxford Anthology of American Literature,* Vol. I. Copyright 1938 by Oxford University Press, Inc. Pp. 677–8.

offence, sure to wreak his vengeance by carrying off their young men and maidens to be sacrificed to his deities. Cortés assured him that he would never consent to such enormities; he had been sent by his sovereign to redress abuses and to punish the oppressor; and, if the Totonacs would be true to him, he would enable them to throw off the detested yoke of the Aztecs.

The cacique added, that the Totonac territory contained about thirty towns and villages; which could muster a hundred thousand warriors, a number much exaggerated. There were other provinces of the empire, he said, where the Aztec rule was equally odious; and between him and the capital lay the warlike republic of Tlascala, which had always maintained its independence of Mexico. The fame of the Spaniards had gone before them, and he was well acquainted with their terrible victory at Tabasco. But still he looked with doubt and alarm to a rupture with "the great Montezuma," as he always styled him; whose armies, on the least provocation, would pour down from the mountain regions of the west, and, rushing over the plains like a whirlwind, sweep off the wretched people to slavery and sacrifice!

Cortés endeavoured to reassure him, by declaring that a single Spaniard was stronger than a host of Aztecs. At the same time, it was desirable to know what nations would co-operate with him, not so much on his account, as theirs, that he might distinguish friend from foe, and know whom he was to spare in this war of extermination. Having raised the confidence of the admiring chief by this comfortable and politic vaunt, he took an affectionate leave, with the assurance that he would shortly return and concert measures for their future operations, when he had visited his ships in the adjoining port, and secured a permanent settlement there.

The intelligence gained by Cortés gave great satisfaction to his mind. It confirmed his former views, and showed, indeed, the interior of the monarchy to be in a state far more distracted than he had supposed. If he had before scarcely shrunk from attacking the Aztec empire in the true spirit of a knight-errant, with his single arm, as it were, what had he now to fear, when one half of the nation could be thus marshalled against the other? In the excitement of the moment, his sanguine spirit kindled with an enthusiasm which overleaped every obstacle. He communicated his own feelings to the officers about him, and, before a blow was struck, they already felt as if the banners of Spain were waving in triumph from the towers of Montezuma! But many a bloody field was to be fought, many a peril and privation to be encountered, before that consummation could be attained.

Taking leave of the hospitable Indian on the following day, the Spaniards took the road to Chiahuitzla, about four leagues distant, near which was the port discovered by Montejo, where their ships were now riding at anchor. They passed through a country of the same rich, voluptuous character as that which they had lately traversed; and arrived early next morning at the Indian town, perched like a fortress on a bold, rocky eminence that commanded the Gulf.

Ending Time:

Hour:_____Minutes:_____Seconds:_____

LITERATURE I—*Cortés Makes an Ally*

Comprehension Check

Indicate whether, according to the article just read, each of the following statements is true or false.

1. T F When Cortés visited the lord of Cempoalla some 500 men accompanied him.
2. T F The mansion of Cempoalla was made of earth and lime.
3. T F The interpreter of Cortés was a beautiful young woman.
4. T F The Totonacs claimed that they could muster 100,000 warriors.
5. T F The Totonacs were subjects of the Spanish.
6. T F The Spaniards were badly defeated at the battle of Tabasco.
7. T F The Totonacs had never heard of the Spaniards before Cortés' visit.
8. T F Cortés threatened the chief with death if the Totonacs did not aid the Spaniards against the Aztecs.
9. T F Cortés felt that he could cause the Indians to revolt against the Aztecs and fight for the Spaniards.
10. T F The Indian countryside was barren and strewn with rocks.

Now check your answers with the key on page 16. Then determine your percentage of comprehension by checking in the table below.

Number of Answers Correct	10	9	8	7	6	5	4	3	2	1
Percentage of Comprehension	100	90	80	70	60	50	40	30	20	10

Reading Rate: In the spaces below fill in the times when you began and finished reading the selection. Subtract the beginning time from the ending time. Now check your rate of reading to the nearest time unit in the table below.

	Hour	Minutes	Seconds
Ending Time:	___	___	___
Beginning Time:	___	___	___
Total Reading Time:	___	___	___

Time	1'00"	1'15"	1'30"	1'45"	2'00"	2'15"	2'30"	2'45"	3'00"
W.P.M.	742	649	556	463	371	337	304	270	237

Time	3'15"	3'30"	3'45"	4'00"	4'15"	4'30"	4'45"	5'00"
W.P.M.	224	211	198	185	176	166	158	148

SCIENCE PRE-TEST

Purpose: To read as quickly as you can and still understand the general content of this selection.

Procedure: Record the time (hour, minutes, seconds) when you begin reading the selection. After reading the selection, again record the time. Then answer the questions related to the selection.

Beginning Time:

Hour: ___ Minutes: ___ Seconds: ___

(798 words)

The Development of Anaesthesia

THE IDEA of producing a local anaesthesia without any general loss of consciousness was never entirely set aside by surgeons. The older attempts to obtain it by compressing the pain nerves with a tourniquet and by the application of cold to the area

about to be operated upon had not been very successful but it was believed that eventually a new and more satisfactory technique would be found. Later this belief was justified by the introduction of cocaine into medical practice. Cocaine is yet another example of a remedy coming from a primitive and ancient source. We owe it to the Incas of Peru who regarded the coca-plant with great veneration and made offerings of its leaves to their Sun God. The priests also made a practice of chewing these leaves and, according to an old legend, they were capable of performing almost incredible feats of endurance whilst under its influence. And quite apart from legend, the modern Peruvians recognized that chewing the leaves of the "divine plant of the Incas" warded off hunger and fatigue. It was the custom in Peru to open up old Inca graves in the hope of recovering from them ancient and precious relics, and whilst doing this the excavators were very liable to develop sore throats due to the inhaling of the fine dust into which the uncovered bodies immediately crumbled on being exposed to the air. In order to guard against these sore throats those who were engaged in the digging usually chewed coca-leaves and it was mainly through this habit of theirs that the notice of European travellers was drawn to the medicinal properties of the coca-plant.

The first man to use cocaine for medical purposes was the Viennese surgeon Koller, who in 1884 discovered that it was of great value as a local anaesthetic in eye operations. But we owe almost all further developments in cocaine anaesthesia to the enterprise and the ingenuity of American surgeons. Solutions of cocaine were first injected into nerve endings by the American surgeon W. S. Halstead (1852), and three years later J. L. Corning introduced the technique known as spinal anaesthesia. This valuable method of employing cocaine consists of injecting it into the spinal canal so that it produces complete anaesthesia of the nerves lying below the level of the injection. The American surgeon, G. W. Crile, combined spinal anaesthesia with general anaesthesia, thereby reducing the shock of an operation. Chemists were not long in discovering the chemical structure of cocaine and for many years they have been synthesizing a number of new compounds of a similar nature to cocaine but much less toxic.

The story of anaesthesia is therefore very closely linked with medical progress in the New World. Not only were American surgeons much quicker to realize the great potentialities of nitrous oxide and ether as general anaesthetics, not only were they more enterprising in developing local anaesthesia than we were, but cocaine, the drug first used in local anaesthesia, came originally from the New World. We also owe to the Incas of Peru a preparation which is now being used on a big scale in conjunction with anaesthetics, the drug known as curare. One of the requirements of the modern surgeon is that the muscles of the patient on whom he is operating should be fully relaxed, and the muscles of modern urbanized man are very seldom in this condition even when he is asleep. Curare possesses the special property of paralyzing the nerve endings in the muscles and when the anaesthetist finds it impossible to obtain a good muscular relaxation by his anaesthetic alone he gives the patient an injection of this drug. It was used long ago by the old hunters of Peru who dipped their arrow heads in the poison because they found that by doing so they lost fewer of their arrows through the wounded prey escaping. The poison acted by being absorbed from the wound into the animal's blood stream and by quickly bringing about a paralysis of its muscles.

The administration of an anaesthetic has now become such a skilled proceeding that anaesthetics is recognized as a specialty in medicine. It is moreover a specialty which is of immense importance to the modern surgeon, who has made such spectacular advances during the last fifty years that he has been able to enter into areas of the body into which his predecessors would not have dared to intrude, into regions such as the brain, the chest cavity, the heart, the lungs and the great blood vessels. This remarkable surgical progress could never have been made had it not been for the parallel advances being made in the specialty of anaesthesia.

Ending Time:

Hour: _____ Minutes: _____ Seconds: _____

SCIENCE I—*The Development of Anaesthesia*

Comprehension Check

Indicate whether, according to the article just read, each of the following statements is true or false.

1. T F Modern surgery has advanced because of anaesthesia.
2. T F Cocaine, an early anaesthetic, was derived from the venom of the cobra.
3. T F The "divine plant of the Incas" was the coca-plant.
4. T F The Incas preserved their dead with fumes from coca leaves.
5. T F Cocaine was first used for medical purposes by the Viennese surgeon Koller.
6. T F Spinal anaesthesia was first developed by an American doctor.
7. T F Surgeons still do not dare to explore the brain and heart.
8. T F American surgeons lagged behind in using nitrous oxide and ether as anaesthetics.
9. T F Curare was first found by the Incas.
10. T F Some medical men devote their career to the study and administration of anaesthetics.

Now check your answers with the key on page 16. Then determine your percentage of comprehension by checking in the table below.

Number of Answers Correct	10	9	8	7	6	5	4	3	2	1
Percentage of Comprehension	100	90	80	70	60	50	40	30	20	10

Reading Rate: In the spaces below fill in the times when you began and finished reading the selection. Subtract the beginning time from the ending time. Now check your rate of reading to the nearest time unit in the table below.

	Hour	Minutes	Seconds
Ending Time:	_____	_____	_____
Beginning Time:	_____	_____	_____
Total Reading Time:	_____	_____	_____

Time	1'00"	1'15"	1'30"	1'45"	2'00"	2'15"	2'30"	2'45"	3'00"
W.P.M.	798	699	598	499	399	365	332	299	266

Time	3'15"	3'30"	3'45"	4'00"	4'15"	4'30"	4'45"	5'00"
W.P.M.	249	233	216	200	190	180	170	160

HISTORY PRE-TEST

Purpose: To read as quickly as you can and still understand the general content of this selection.

Procedure: Record the time (hour, minutes, seconds) when you begin reading the selection. After reading the selection, again record the time. Then answer the questions related to the selection.

Beginning Time:

Hour: _____ Minutes: _____ Seconds: _____

(880 words)

Washington, Farmer-President

WASHINGTON ACCEPTED the Presidency with great reluctance. It had been his hope and wish to spend the remainder of his days at Mount Vernon as a scientific farmer, improving American husbandry by experiment and example. Washington studied the best works on the subject, corresponded with English experts such as Arthur Young, imported improved implements, and applied new methods. Tobacco culture, which had exhausted the soil of Tidewater Virginia, was relinquished at Mount Vernon as early as 1765. Wheat, flax, and root crops were substituted for corn, pasturage was increased, a five-year rotation of crops adopted, and sheep folded on turnips or clover.

Mount Vernon, unlike the modern "gentleman's country estate" that is supported by income from other sources, supported its proprietor; and Washington's relation to it was more like that of an industrial manager to his plant. Washington inherited an estate of 2500 acres and added about 5500 more, until Mount Vernon stretched ten miles along the broad Potomac. The 3500 acres under cultivation around 1790 were divided by tracts of woodland into separate farms,

Samuel Eliot Morison and Henry Steele Commager. *The Growth of the American Republic,* 4th ed. Copyright 1950 by Oxford University Press, Inc. Pp. 325–7.

each with its own force of slaves and an overseer, who must report weekly how he had employed every hand. There were great wooden barns, with cow stables and spacious threshing-floors. The pastures, enclosed by worm fences, produced a thin, poor turf in that land of hot, dry summers. Brood-mares and blooded stallions occupied the best watered of them. Royal Gift, a fifteen-hand jackass presented by the King of Spain, had a special paddock and groom, as befitted the ancestor of the American army mule. The cattle were undersized and of low breed; the hogs ran at large through the woodlands, affording illicit sport for a pack of French boar-hounds, an unwelcome gift from Lafayette.

Mount Vernon was an industrial as well as an agricultural unit. There were slave blacksmiths, carpenters, and even bricklayers; a cider press and a still-house, where excellent rye and Bourbon whisky were made, and sold in barrels made by plantation Negroes from home-grown oak. Herring and shad fisheries in the Potomac provided food for the slaves; a grist-mill turned Washington's improved strain of wheat into the finest grade of flour, which was taken to market in his own schooner. There was a weaving-shed, where a dozen different textiles were produced from local wool and flax, and West India cotton. Picture Washington rising at sunrise, breakfasting at seven, and superintending from the saddle the work on his several farms, frequently dismounting and stripping his coat to demonstrate with his strong back and large, capable hands how things should be done. His good lady, in the meantime, would be directing the work of a large force of household slaves, and helping to cut and piece home-woven cloth for the Negroes. Dinner at three ended the day's work in the field; but there were usually accounts and problems enough to occupy the master until supper.

For recreation there was fox-hunting with his own and his neighbors' packs; taking toll of the great flights of wild duck, goose, and pigeon; dancing assemblies at Alexandria. A constant stream of relations and friends flowed through the mansion house, few distinguished travelers came South unprovided with a letter to the great man, and no gentleman could be turned away from his door. The guests, in fact, ate up most of the increase not consumed by the slaves, whose children Washington was too humane to sell away from their parents.

This was the life that Washington loved, and in which he hoped to spend his declining years. No detail was too small for his attention, no slave too humble to attract his interest, no blight too devastating to command his patience. Even on his campaigns, and in the Presidency, he would write sixteen-page letters of instruction to his overseers; and one suspects that, like Sir Robert Walpole, he read their reports before he turned to the affairs of state. "The more I am acquainted with agricultural affairs, the better I am pleased with them," he wrote to Arthur Young in 1788. "How much more delightful . . . is the task of making improvements in the earth than all the vain glory which can be acquired from ravaging it by the most uninterrupted career of conquests."

The qualities that made Washington the first farmer and the first soldier in America also made him the first statesman. As landed proprietor no less than as commander-in-chief, he had shown executive ability, the power of planning for a distant end, and a capacity for taking infinite pains. Neither drought nor defeat, nor, as it proved, political abuse, could turn him from a course that he discerned to be proper and right. In describing himself as one who inherited "inferior endowments from nature," Washington was too modest; but we shall underestimate the difficulties of his task if we forget that his superiority lay in character, not in talents. He had the power of inspiring respect and trust, but not the gift of popularity; directness but not adroitness; fortitude rather than flexibility; the power to think things through, not quick perception; a natural presence and dignity, but none of that brisk assertiveness that has often given inferior men greater political influence. The mask of dignity and reserve that concealed his inner life came from shyness, humility, and stoical self-control. A warm heart was revealed in numerous kindly acts to his dependents and subordinates. And beneath the cool surface of him there glowed a fire that under provocation would burst forth in immoderate laughter, astounding oaths, or Olympian anger.

Ending Time:

Hour: _____ Minutes: _____ Seconds: _____

HISTORY I—*Washington, Farmer-President*

Comprehension Check

Indicate whether, according to the selection just read, each of the following statements is true or false.

1. T F Washington was eager to become President after his hard life as a soldier and farmer.
2. T F Tobacco was the principal crop at Mount Vernon after 1765.
3. T F Mount Vernon was able to support its proprietor.
4. T F Washington was given Mount Vernon by a grateful government.
5. T F Mount Vernon was an industrial as well as agricultural center.

6. T F Washington found it impossible to grow a high quality grain.
7. T F Mrs. Washington led a life of leisure.
8. T F Washington was proud and harsh with his slaves.
9. T F Washington was probably more interested in his farm than in affairs of government.
10. T F Washington is considered to have been a man of character rather than one who had great talents.

Now check your answers with the key on page 16. Then determine your percentage of comprehension by checking in the table below.

Number of Answers Correct	10	9	8	7	6	5	4	3	2	1
Percentage of Comprehension	100	90	80	70	60	50	40	30	20	10

Reading Rate: In the spaces below fill in the times when you began and finished reading the selection. Subtract the beginning time from the ending time. Now check your rate of reading to the nearest time unit in the table below.

	Hour	Minutes	Seconds
Ending Time:	_____	_____	_____
Beginning Time:	_____	_____	_____
Total Reading Time:		_____	_____

Time	1'00"	1'15"	1'30"	1'45"	2'00"	2'15"	2'30"	2'45"	3'00"
W.P.M.	880	770	660	550	440	403	366	330	293

Time	3'15"	3'30"	3'45"	4'00"	4'15"	4'30"	4'45"	5'00"
W.P.M.	274	256	238	220	209	198	187	176

PSYCHOLOGY PRE-TEST

(871 words)

Purpose: To read as quickly as you can and still understand the general content of this selection.

Procedure: Record the time (hour, minutes, seconds) when you begin reading the selection. After reading the selection, again record the time. Then answer the questions related to the selection.

Beginning Time:

Hour: _____ Minutes: _____ Seconds: _____

Interests

THE PRIMARY basis upon which children select interests is that of the emotional appeal that is felt. Their likes and dislikes are personal, and an interest must produce satisfactions and be consistent with their personal aims in order to be acceptable. If unpleasant mental effort makes pursuit of

Robert A. Davis. *Educational Psychology.* Copyright 1948 by McGraw-Hill Book Co., Inc. Pp. 98–103.

an intellectual interest dissatisfying, preference is likely to be given to substituted interests in which physical activity predominates.

Many interests are associated with wish fulfillment. Individuals constantly seek experiences that afford them success. Their standards of success vary but are usually associated with desire for personal recognition or maintenance of self-esteem. The experiences through which success is sought may be obtained through active interests, in which one is personally engaged in the pursuit of an interest. Playing tennis or building boats may be considered active interests. The experiences of others may be utilized vicariously, as in inactive or passive interests, from which the emotional effect may be felt through mental participation. Reading a book or watching a tennis match constitutes a passive interest. Interests may be variously motivated. Several motives may operate simultaneously; but although individuals may be aware of their preferences for certain activities, they are seldom conscious of the purposes that such activities serve.

A child is seeking satisfaction of a broad purpose in selecting one game rather than another because of particularly happy relationships with a certain group of playmates. His interest in the game may be both in the desire to excel in the skill involved and in enjoying the satisfaction of being socially acceptable. He may even participate solely because his refusal might be socially offensive. Certain individual interests may have mildly competitive aspects, as in postage-stamp collecting, at which the child hopes to acquire those items which are more valuable and rare than those of other children. One may become interested in taking long walks because of desire to be alone with his thoughts, the pleasantness of places he may visit, or the beneficial effects of fresh air and exercise. The individual may be unaware that he is relieving himself of many tensions and is making an emotional as well as physiological adjustment.

The exploratory or imitative character of many interests constitutes a form of adaptive activity. A little girl plays school in an investigation of her ability at adult imitation. A boy may construct a miniature pulpit of scrap lumber and play minister as an experiment in realism. The amateur photographer adheres to prescribed techniques in order to obtain pleasurable success in results comparable with those of professional photographers. Imitation extends beyond blind acceptance of behavior patterns of other persons into desire for satisfactions to be derived from success in duplicating their performance.

The extent to which one identifies himself with characters in movies or reading and obtains vicarious satisfactions depends largely upon the individual, whose responses may be subjective or highly objective. Some individuals are moved by scenes of suffering or sorrow to the extent of shedding tears. Others may regard the performance as oversentimental and ridiculous. Without leaving his easy chair one may, through reading, enjoy many of the experiences of traveling in foreign countries or being emotionally in rapport with the characters in a work of fiction. One may harmlessly experience the thrills of danger by identifying himself with a character in a movie or a story whose performance at daring deeds he might be reluctant to imitate in actual life.

People attend movies or read from very obscure motives, which are in most cases unknown to them. These interests may be sought simply to relieve boredom or to obtain the pleasure that is habitually obtained from witnessing favorite actors or reading works by certain authors and enjoying their characteristic styles. Painters, artists, writers, and musicians make their work capable of arousing in others the emotions that they themselves experience. The fact that individuals make different interpretations of identical situations accounts for the variable effects of a movie or a book.

Movies, in particular, become an interest of many people because of the completeness of detail with which they may enjoy a different type of life from that which they experience daily. As a rule, the environment depicted is on a higher plane from that of their own everyday experiences. The tendency of movies to glorify even the most lowly activities of life possesses democratic appeal. Individuals may readily discover means of escape from their own drab surroundings and annoyances by imagining that they themselves are performing the activities that they are witnessing.

A wide variety of well-selected interests is important to a child's emotional life as a means of utilizing the flow of energy that dissatisfying situations generate. In cases in which a child is frustrated by lack of success in the classroom or is distressed by certain conditions in his home, it is highly important that his pent-up emotions find opportunity for wholesome expression. A game of baseball after school or a hike into the woods with companions affords opportunity to maintain emotional poise. The more active a child is in pursuit of a variety of constructive interests, the wider the range of possibilities for making adequate personal adjustments.

Ending Time:

Hour: _____ Minutes: _____ Seconds: _____

PSYCHOLOGY I—*Interests*

Comprehension Check

Indicate whether, according to the selection just read, each of the following is true or false.

1. T F Children select interests primarily on the basis of emotional appeal.
2. T F In order to be acceptable to an individual an interest must produce satisfaction.
3. T F For each interest there is a single motivating force.
4. T F A child who does not excel in a game will always discontinue participation in that game.
5. T F Adults, unlike children, seldom enter into an activity without an awareness of the motivation lying behind their interest in the activity.
6. T F Social acceptance provides a less strong motivational drive to participate in an activity than does interest.
7. T F Many interests are associated with wish fulfillments.
8. T F A wide variety of well-selected interests is considered more desirable than a few such interests.
9. T F Movies serve as an undesirable means of escape because of their unrealistic portrayal of everyday experiences.
10. T F Individuals may be aware of their preferences for certain activities, but are seldom conscious of the purposes that such activities serve.

Now check your answers with the key on page 16. Then determine your percentage of comprehension by checking in the table below.

Number of Answers Correct	10	9	8	7	6	5	4	3	2	1
Percentage of Comprehension	100	90	80	70	60	50	40	30	20	10

Reading Rate: In the spaces below fill in the times when you began and finished reading the selection. Subtract the beginning time from the ending time. Now check your rate of reading to the nearest time unit in the table below.

	Hour	Minutes	Seconds
Ending Time:	_____	_____	_____
Beginning Time:	_____	_____	_____
Total Reading Time:	_____	_____	_____

Time	1'00"	1'15"	1'30"	1'45"	2'00"	2'15"	2'30"	2'45"
W.P.M.	871	697	580	497	435	388	349	318

Time	3'00"	3'15"	3'30"	3'45"	4'00"	4'15"	4'30"	4'45"	5'00"
W.P.M.	290	269	249	232	217	205	194	183	174

Comprehension Check Key

A. **NARRATIVE**—*Rest Stop for the Sanderlings*

   1-T, 2-F, 3-T, 4-F, 5-T, 6-T, 7-F, 8-T, 9-F, 10-T

B. **LITERATURE**—*Cortés Makes an Ally*

   1-F, 2-F, 3-T, 4-F, 5-T, 6-F, 7-T, 8-T, 9-F, 10-F

C. **SCIENCE**—*The Development of Anaesthesia*

   1-T, 2-F, 3-T, 4-F, 5-T, 6-T, 7-F, 8-F, 9-T, 10-T

D. **HISTORY**—*Washington, Farmer-President*

   1-F, 2-F, 3-T, 4-F, 5-T, 6-F, 7-F, 8-F, 9-T, 10-T

E. **PSYCHOLOGY**—*Interests*

   1-T, 2-T, 3-F, 4-F, 5-F, 6-F, 7-T, 8-T, 9-F, 10-T

Summary of Flexibility Tests

Highest Rate	_____
Lowest Rate	_____
Range of Reading Rate	_____

YOU HAVE read five selections and determined your reading rate and percentage of comprehension for each. In the table below enter the information from each of these selections.

Selection	Rate (W.P.M.)	Comprehension Percentage
1. Rest Stop for the Sanderlings		
2. Cortés Makes an Ally		
3. The Development of Anaesthesia		
4. Washington, Farmer-President		
5. Interests		
Average Rate & Comprehension for five selections		

Completing the next three steps will help provide you with a clearer picture of your reading flexibility.

1. Determine your average reading rate and comprehension for the five selections and enter these figures in the spaces provided in the table. To do this add all of the reading rate figures and all the figures for percentage of comprehension. Then divide each of the resulting total figures by five.

2. Determine your range of reading rate by subtracting the lowest of the five reading rates from the highest of the five rates. This figure will give you an indication of the degree of flexibility with which you read.

Where in the following table of flexibility does your range of reading rate place you?

Range of Rate*	Nature of Flexibility
25–50	Very Poor
50–100	Poor to Fair
100–125	Fair to Good
125–150	Good
150–200	Very Good
200–300	Excellent
300–	Outstanding

3. On the graph on the next page plot your reading rate figures for each of the five kinds of material you have just read. This will give you a graphic picture of your range of reading rate (flexibility) and a comparison with the figures obtained by other readers.

If you are an efficient and skilled reader your line on the graph should resemble "A"—high in Narrative, low in Science, average in History and Psychology. If it resembles "C" then you are a *slow,* inflexible reader. If it resembles "B" you are a *fast* and inflexible reader. If your comprehension is 100 per cent on all selections you have probably read too slowly. If it is 70 per cent and below you need to slow up. Remember, flexibility is the important factor in improvement, not speed alone.

Flexibility in reading is considered to be that aspect of reading which causes the reader to be both adaptable and versatile. The flexible reader adapts his reading to the purpose with which he approaches the printed page, the difficulty level of the material, and the degree of his own familiarity with the subject of the material. The goal of a flexible reader is to obtain the desired degree of understanding with the greatest amount of efficiency.

* Rapid rate accompanied by below 80 per cent comprehension or a feeling on the part of the reader that he did not understand what he was reading would, of course, not be a valid basis for comment.

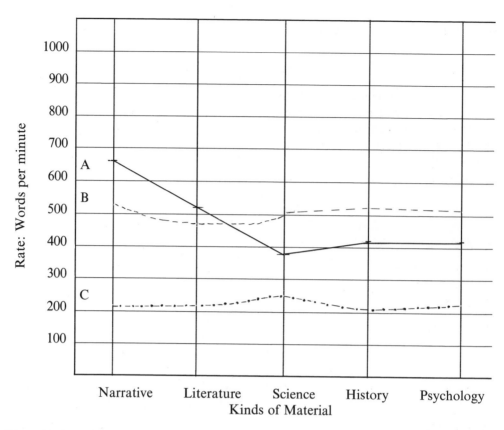

Lines "A" and "C" on the graph may take on added meaning to you if you look at them again with the knowledge that they represent actual results from this same test administered to college freshmen. Line "C" shows average rates obtained by freshmen on the Flexibility Pre-Test. Line "A" shows average rates obtained on the Flexibility Post-Test by these same freshmen students at the end of a one-semester course in improving reading and study skills. With which line do your rates most closely compare?

VOCABULARY PRE-TEST

Roots of Words

HOW WELL do you know the important roots of English words? Below are listed ten Latin and ten Greek roots which are the base for many English words. Write a meaning for each root and list at least two words that are derived from each root.

Latin root	*Meaning*	*English words*
1. facio	_____	_____
2. duco	_____	_____
3. tendo	_____	_____
4. fero	_____	_____

Latin root	Meaning	English words
5. aqua	_____	_____
6. bene	_____	_____
7. frater	_____	_____
8. loquor	_____	_____
9. porto	_____	_____
10. primus	_____	_____

Greek root	Meaning	English words
1. autos	_____	_____
2. ge	_____	_____
3. homos	_____	_____
4. octo	_____	_____
5. philos	_____	_____
6. phobos	_____	_____
7. phone	_____	_____
8. pseudos	_____	_____
9. sophos	_____	_____
10. theos	_____	_____

Prefixes

Do you know the meaning of the following prefixes? Write what each prefix means to you and then write two words in which the prefix appears.

Prefix	Meaning	Words
1. con	_____	_____
2. ad	_____	_____
3. re	_____	_____
4. in	_____	_____
5. un	_____	_____
6. be	_____	_____
7. ab	_____	_____
8. sur	_____	_____
9. dis	_____	_____
10. pro	_____	_____

Suffixes

Do you know the meaning of the following suffixes? Write what each suffix means to you and then write two words in which the suffix appears.

Suffix	Meaning	Words
1. able	_____	_____
2. ation	_____	_____
3. en	_____	_____

Suffix	Meaning	Words
4. fy	_____	_____
5. ice	_____	_____
6. ly	_____	_____
7. or	_____	_____
8. ous	_____	_____
9. tude	_____	_____
10. ure	_____	_____

Antonyms

WORDS that have a meaning opposite to other words are called antonyms. In each of the rows below, you will find *one* word that means the opposite of the key word. Underline this word or antonym.

Key Word

1. agog	eager aloof avid athirst
2. mitigate	allay relieve intensify lighten
3. debilitate	invigorate undermine sap enfeeble
4. baleful	malefic sinister malign benign
5. fecund	barren fruitful yielding prolific
6. precise	accurate loose nice correct
7. arid	verdant dry desiccated barren
8. laconic	verbose terse pithy succinct
9. redundant	wordy concise verbose diffuse
10. ascetic	austere sybaritic disciplined severe

Synonyms

OUR language is rich in descriptive words. Words that mean the same or about the same as other words are called synonyms.

In each row of words below you will find three that are synonyms of the key word and one that is not. Underline in each row the synonyms of the key word.

Key Word

1. abet	incite deter foment instigate
2. mortal	venial deadly fatal lethal
3. heterogeneous	motley uniform assorted diverse
4. enmity	antipathy amity rancor animus
5. choleric	testy irascible imperturbable cross
6. avid	agog averse eager anxious
7. pallid	pale wan livid ashen
8. quack	impostor charlatan faker lawyer
9. rotund	angular portly corpulent stout
10. passive	inert operative idle supine

KEY TO VOCABULARY PRE-TEST

Roots of Words

SEVERAL words are listed under English words for each group. The student may list other words than these however. The words he lists should be checked for accuracy in the dictionary.

Latin root	*Meaning*	*English words*
1. facio	do or make	facility, factory
2. duco	lead, bring forward	deduce, abduct, viaduct
3. tendo	stretch	extend, tension
4. fero	bear or carry	fertile, transfer
5. aqua	water	aquarium, aquatic
6. bene	well	benefit, beneficial
7. frater	brother	fraternity, fraternize
8. loquor	speak	loquacious, eloquent
9. porto	carry	porter, transport
10. primus	first	prime, primary

Greek root	*Meaning*	*English words*
1. autos	self	autobiography, automatic
2. geo	earth	geography, geology
3. homos	alike	homonym, homogeneous
4. octo	eight	octogon, octave
5. philos	friend, lover	philosopher, philanthropy
6. phobos	fear	phobia, Anglophobia
7. phone	sound	telephone, phonograph
8. pseudes	false	pseudonym, pseudomorph
9. sophos	wise	sophomore, philosopher
10. theos	God	theology, theism

Prefixes

UNDER the column headed Words, a few words containing the prefix are given. There are many others, of course, and if the student lists them they should be checked in the dictionary.

Prefix	*Meaning*	*Words*
1. con	with	concur, concord
2. ad	to, toward	admit, admire
3. re	again, back	return, re-enter
4. in	into, not	inbred, insincere
5. un	not	unable, unwilling
6. be	make, against	befoul, bedim
7. ab	from, away, off	abnormal
8. sur	over, super.	surpass, surcharge
9. dis	away, removal	dismiss, disembark
10. pro	before in place, time, order, rank	pronoun, propel

Suffixes

UNDER the column headed Words, a few words containing the suffix are given. There are many others, of course, and if the student lists them they should be checked in the dictionary.

Suffix	*Meaning*	*Words*
1. able	having the quality, capacity, or fitness	communicable, acceptable
2. ation	act or doing, state of being	transportation, civilization
3. en	made of	wooden, golden
4. fy	to make, form into	beautify, purify
5. ice	act, quality, condition	service, novice
6. ly	like in appearance, manner, nature	fatherly, queenly
7. or	state or quality of, one who	ardor, executor
8. ous	full of, having qualities of	joyous, gracious
9. tude	state, condition, quality	magnitude, gratitude
10. ure	act, process, or being	culture, legislature

Antonyms

THE antonym to the key word is underlined.

Key Word

1. agog — eager <u>aloof</u> avid athirst
2. mitigate — allay relieve <u>intensify</u> lighten
3. debilitate — <u>invigorate</u> undermine sap enfeeble
4. baleful — malefic sinister malign <u>benign</u>
5. fecund — <u>barren</u> fruitful yielding prolific
6. precise — accurate <u>loose</u> nice correct
7. arid — <u>verdant</u> dry desiccated barren
8. laconic — <u>verbose</u> terse pithy succinct
9. redundant — wordy <u>concise</u> verbose diffuse
10. ascetic — austere <u>sybaritic</u> disciplined severe

Synonyms

THE synonyms of the key word are underlined.

Key Word

1. abet — <u>incite</u> deter <u>foment</u> <u>instigate</u>
2. mortal — venial <u>deadly</u> <u>fatal</u> <u>lethal</u>
3. heterogeneous — <u>motley</u> uniform <u>assorted</u> <u>diverse</u>
4. enmity — <u>antipathy</u> amity <u>rancor</u> <u>animus</u>
5. choleric — <u>testy</u> <u>irascible</u> imperturbable <u>cross</u>
6. avid — <u>agog</u> averse <u>eager</u> <u>anxious</u>
7. pallid — <u>pale</u> <u>wan</u> livid <u>ashen</u>
8. quack — <u>impostor</u> <u>charlatan</u> <u>faker</u> lawyer
9. rotund — angular <u>portly</u> <u>corpulent</u> <u>stout</u>
10. passive — <u>inert</u> operative <u>idle</u> <u>supine</u>

STUDY SKILLS CHECK LIST

FOLLOWING IS a list of statements concerning study skills and practices. Some of these reflect good and some poor practices. The purpose of this check list is to help you assess your present study methods and procedures in respect to these various practices.

Read and consider each statement. Then place a check mark in the appropriate column opposite that statement as it applies to you.

	YES (This is Usually True)	NO (This is Seldom True)

Study Habits and Facilities

1. I have a quiet, well-lighted, and heated place in which to study.

2. I study in the same place each day.

3. I *make* a work-study schedule to use as a guide to help utilize my time effectively.

4. I *follow* a work-study schedule.

5. I arrange my study schedule so that I study my most difficult subject first.

6. I study in several short periods rather than in a few prolonged sessions.

7. I review all material covered in each course at least once weekly.

8 I have a tendency to "day-dream" when trying to study.

Reading

9. I skim over a reading assignment before studying it.

10 I have to reread materials several times in order to understand their meaning.

11 I have difficulty in identifying the main idea of a passage.

12 I pronounce words to myself when I read.

13. I read various kinds of materials for different purposes at different rates.

	YES (This is Usually True)	NO (This is Seldom True)
14 I have difficulty in understanding and remembering what I read.		
15. I read numerous books and articles in addition to class assignments (at least one book per month).		

Note Taking

16. I take notes in an outline form.		
17 My notes are disorganized and I have trouble understanding them when I study.		
18 I try to take down everything the professor says when I take notes.		
19 I recopy my notes after taking them in a lecture.		
20 I take my lecture notes in shorthand.		
21. I look over and edit my notes after class.		
22. I keep my notes in one loose-leaf notebook on 8½ x 11 paper.		

Examinations

23. I have little or no trouble in taking an examination and getting a good grade.		
24. I do the more difficult items on an examination first.		
25 I "freeze-up" when I enter an examination.		
26. I leave items on an examination which I can not answer immediately and go back to them later.		
27. I outline answers to essay-type questions before starting to write.		
28. I "survey" or skim over the entire examination before starting to answer any questions.		
29. I check over returned examinations to determine where and why I lost credit.		

All of the items in the preceding check list are considered to be good practices except items 8, 10, 11, 12, 14, 17, 18, 19, 20, and 25. (You will notice that these items do not have periods after the number). Thus to have a perfect "score" on this check list you should have marked each of these ten items in the "no" column. All others should be marked "yes."

If you have checked the "yes" column for any poor practices, or if you have checked the "no" column for any of the good practices, place a circle around the number of that item. Each encircled item represents a skill or practice which you should include for consideration in your program for improving reading and study skills.

Note each of the skills and the area in which you need to improve. Listed below, under the four areas covered in this check list, are specific sources which will be helpful in improving those skills in which you may be weak. Read the selection or selections suggested. Copies of the book suggested will probably be available in your college library or reading center.

Study Habits and Facilities

1. Francis P. Robinson. *Effective Study,* Harper & Brothers, New York, 1946.
   Project IV—"Skills in Attack and Concentration," pp. 55–69
2. C. G. Wrenn and R. P. Larsen. *Studying Effectively*, Stanford University Press, Stanford, Calif., 1957.
   "Planning Your Work," pp. 5–9
   "Increasing Your Ability To Concentrate," pp. 19–21

3. Max Meenes. *Studying and Learning,* Random House, New York, 1954.
   "Study Motivation," pp. 6–20

Reading

1. Leonard S. Braam and William D. Sheldon. *Developing Efficient Reading,* Oxford University Press, Inc., New York, 1959.
   "Becoming an Efficient Reader," pp. 29–31
   "Familiarity," pp. 44–45
   "Improving Comprehension," p. 69
   "A Week of Reading at College," pp. 97–99

Note Taking

1. Francis P. Robinson. *Effective Study,* Harper & Brothers, New York, 1946.
   "Improving Ability To Handle Lectures," pp. 94–96
2. C. G. Wrenn and R. P. Larsen. *Studying Effectively,* Stanford University Press, Stanford, Calif., 1957.
   "Taking Notes," pp. 21–23

Examinations

1. Francis P. Robinson. *Effective Study,* Harper & Brothers, New York, 1946.
   Project III—"Effective Skill in Examinations," pp. 43–54
2. C. G. Wrenn and R. P. Larsen. *Studying Effectively,* Stanford University Press, Stanford, Calif., 1957.
   "Preparing for and Taking Examinations," pp. 23–27

II—Efficient Reading

BECOMING AN EFFICIENT READER

READING IS involved in an extremely high percentage of a student's daily activities. It is important for academic success that reading, like other learning tasks, be carried out in the most efficient manner.

How can the college student become more efficient in reading? Part of the answer has been provided by the authors of *Developing Efficient Reading.* This book has been designed for the purpose of helping the college student become a more efficient reader.

It is not enough for one merely to read faster. Increase in speed alone can result in less efficient reading due to a loss in comprehension. An efficient style of reading requires *flexibility,* that is, the ability to shift from a high to a low rate of speed according to the purpose for which reading is to be done. A flexible reading rate results from a consideration of the purpose for which the reading is being done and the degree to which the reader is already familiar with the subject of the material being read. Flexibility is also affected by differences in levels of difficulty in the ideas, concepts, vocabulary, and style of material.

The authors of this book have developed their philosophy of reading through experience and research with college students. We define reading as the interpretation of written materials. This interpretation is based on the ability of the reader to understand the purpose of the author as well as what the author is saying. Reading is not only a rapid recognition of verbal symbols but also an understanding of the thoughts and ideas for which they stand. The exercises in this book follow the pattern suggested by this belief.

Through investigation and observation the authors have found that poor or inadequate readers exhibit common and observable shortcomings, which are generally directly opposite to the characteristics of good readers.

The poor reader usually has an inadequate vocabulary. He reads in a word-by-word fashion. Often he lacks a clear-cut purpose for reading. The poor reader approaches his reading tasks in an inflexible manner. One of his most serious problems is his lack of critical reaction to what he reads. Little or no "extra-curricular" reading is done by the inadequate reader. He seems unable to apply various techniques of reading such as skimming and careful reading when he is satisfying study requirements. Lastly, his comprehension of what he reads is at a low level and his recall of the material most inadequate.

A good reader, on the other hand, has very different characteristics. He has a large vocabulary, reads in phrases, is guided by a clear-cut purpose, and has a flexible approach to his reading. He thinks critically about what he reads, applies various techniques of reading during study, reads widely on many topics, and usually comprehends what he reads on a high level.

To become an efficient reader, it is necessary to consider three things. First, the *purpose* for reading must be determined. Second, the degree of *familiarity* with, or amount of prior knowledge of, the subject under consideration must be weighed. Third, the *difficulty level* of the material must be assessed.

Consideration of these three factors that affect a person's reading will determine the type of reading to be done. In general there are four types of reading—(1) Study-type, (2) Careful, (3) Rapid, and (4) Skimming. These vary in rate from the slow study-type to extremely fast skimming.

Study-type reading is applied, for example, when dealing with a textbook assignment which must be mastered and thoroughly understood.

Careful reading would be used when a less complete understanding is required. This type of reading is particularly well-suited to situations in which a person is reading for personal appreciation or when one wishes to be able to report on the material in some detail to another individual.

Rapid reading is often used in the reading of novels or other leisure reading when a person wishes to cover material completely, but less thoroughly or intensively than is done with either study or careful reading. Rapid reading is used when reviewing material that has been read previously. Because the material has been read once and is therefore fairly familiar, one's memory can be refreshed easily by rapid reading.

Skimming, the fourth type of reading, is a highly specialized type of reading. Efficient readers consider it to be their most valuable reading skill. On the other hand, less efficient readers consider it a dangerous practice. This feeling arises from a lack of understanding of the purpose and application of skimming.

The efficient reader cannot afford to exclude skimming from his reading skills. It is considered the key reading skill necessary for flexible reading. Skimming provides the truly flexible reader with his great range of reading rate, permitting him to fluctuate from 100 word per minute study-type reading to a 1,000 or more word per minute skimming rate.

What is skimming? Skimming is a type of reading in which printed material is covered in an extremely rapid manner. Its most common applications are for such purposes as to rapidly locate information, i.e. names, dates, or specific ideas; to locate the answer to a specific question; to find a reference; to determine the general idea or content of material in order to refresh one's memory; to determine whether the material is worth reading more slowly or carefully; to ascertain whether or not there are any new or useful ideas; to get a general overview of material before it is read more carefully or studied.

What effect does skimming have upon comprehension? Some individuals avoid skimming for fear of a loss of comprehension. Such people do not understand the application of skimming. They fail to realize that the type of reading employed is determined by the reader's purpose, and that skimming is not an appropriate approach to reading in every case. Every purpose for reading does not require or result in complete understanding of material read. If the reader's purpose is to master completely the contents of an article or a chapter in a book he would probably need to apply a slow study-type reading (although the efficient reader would first skim through this material to determine its general content, appropriateness, etc.). Accompanying each purpose for reading must be a consideration of how much the reader already knows about the subject and to what degree he must comprehend the contents of the material.

The efficient reader is aware also that he can intersperse his careful or study-type reading with skimming. When he encounters passages of little importance in relation to his purpose, or when he encounters sections which contain information or ideas already well known, he skims through these quickly. When he encounters passages containing new or difficult ideas he reverts to his study-type reading to be sure he masters their contents.

How do people skim? Photographs of eye movements during skimming reveal that except for the fact that fixations of the reader's eyes are fewer and farther apart there is no rigid pattern or procedure for skimming. Some individuals read only the first and/or last sentence in each paragraph. Some employ a simultaneously horizontal and vertical (diagonal) pattern through a paragraph or down a page. Some are able to let their eyes fall down the center of the column or page of print. Others do not have these uniform approaches, but seem to skip and jump across and down a page, and occasionally even return momentarily to sections already covered. In all instances, however, the reader is actively looking as he skims for key words, phrases, or ideas.

Although it requires concentrated practice, the art of skimming can be effectively developed. Many people have developed phenomenal rates of skimming (2,000–3,000 words per minute) while maintaining extremely high levels of comprehension. Such individuals are not in any sense "freaks." They are quite ordinary intelligent people who have developed the characteristics and skills of the good reader through conscientious practice.

It should be pointed out that there is no one rate which can be designated as appropriate for any of the four types of reading mentioned here. Reading rate will depend upon purpose, familiarity, and difficulty level—as well as the reader's own abilities.

It should also be emphasized that the rate at which an efficient reader covers written material will vary. Within any single piece of material he will find some sections that will warrant skimming while others will be such that he may find it necessary to apply a study-type of reading in order to achieve adequate understanding.

How can efficient reading be developed? The reading selections and discussion that follow are designed to help you develop your reading skill, your ability to discern the three factors affecting your reading, and your ability to select an appropriate type of reading.

Purpose for Reading

READING MUST be purposeful. In general, there are four common purposes for which college reading is done.

1. To obtain an over-all understanding of the main idea involved in the material.

2. To find a date, place, or specific fact.

3. To obtain such an understanding of the material that it can be recalled in logical sequence with some degree of success.

4. To determine the author's slant, purpose, the facts presented, and how they agree with or differ from what you already know or think about the subject discussed.

Let us now take a look at each of these purposes in more detail with illustrations of each.

MAIN IDEAS

GETTING an over-all understanding of the material presented in a reading selection involves reading to determine the main idea of the material or to answer the question: "What is the chapter about?"

The following two exercises will serve to illustrate this purpose for reading. Selections numbered 1 and 2 have been provided to give you practice in reading for the purpose of locating the main idea. Read each selection as rapidly as possible to locate or identify its main idea. After reading each selection, write out the main idea in your own words in the space provided. Use complete sentences. Next compare your main ideas with those on page 32.

SELECTION 1

Purpose: To read to get an over-all understanding of the material.

Procedure: Read the selection carefully in order to answer the question: "What is this selection about?"

(162 words)

The Country Store

THROUGH ALL the years of its long life, there was little system or order in the country store. A great deal of time was wasted in looking for articles that were not in place, or had no place. Often the customer could find what he wanted more successfully than the

Gerald Carson, *The Old Country Store.* Copyright 1954 by Oxford University Press, Inc. P. 14.

merchant himself—an early version of self-service. Flies swarmed around the molasses barrel and there was never a mosquito bar to keep them off. There was tea in chests, packed in lead foil, and straw matting with strange markings; rice and coffee spilling out on the floor where a bag showed a rent; rum and brandy; harness and whale oil. The air was thick with an all-embracing odor, an aroma composed of dry herbs and wet dogs, of strong tobacco, green hides, and raw humanity. This redolence was to become famous in the annals of the country store as the assortment of goods grew wider and the smells more complex.

Main Idea: _____

_____

_____

Check the key and compare your main idea with the one selected by the author.

SELECTION 2

Purpose: To read to get an over-all understanding of the material

Procedure: Read the selection carefully in order to answer the question: "What is this selection about?"

(119 words)

Alsace

THE PEOPLE of Alsace call their land a serene and smiling place, though wars have been fought for its possession since the time, two thousand years ago, when Julius Caesar came up from the south, leading his well-trained legions into battle against the Germans, invading from the north. Later Charlemagne's grandsons waged war against each other for this same land. And from time to time, all through the years, armies have marched in from one direction and another, from Sweden and from Spain,

From the book *All Men Are Brothers* by Charlie May Simon. Copyright, ©, 1956 by E. P. Dutton & Co., Inc. Reprinted by permission of the publishers. P. 21.

from Italy, Hungary, Germany and from France itself. Each laid claim to the place and to the people, fighting first with spears and bows and arrows, and then with guns, cannons and bombs.

Main Idea: _____

_____

_____

Check the key below and compare your main idea with the one selected by the author.

Key to Selections 1 and 2—Main Ideas

Selection 1—The Country Store
A description of the disorder of the country store.

Selection 2—Alsace
Alsace has been a battle ground for centuries.

SPECIFIC DETAILS

The second purpose for reading (as listed on page 31) is to identify a specific detail such as a date, place, or certain fact. Selections numbered 3 and 4 have been provided to give you practice in reading rapidly to locate the answer to a specific question.

SELECTION 3

Purpose: To locate specific details as rapidly as possible.

Procedure: Read or skim the selection to locate as quickly as possible the answer to the following question: "What barrier to flying has been removed and what barrier has not been removed?"

(232 words)

High Speed Flight

AVIATION MEN firmly believe they can overcome whatever obstacles arise in connection with sound turbulence. They feel confident that they can correct methods of control, strengthen the aircraft, provide sufficient safety factors, and make other possible adjustments necessary for flying at hypersonic speeds. They proceed with caution, but they have no fear of the now familiar sonic wall or any future multiple of it.

They do not feel the same confidence, however, about another much more formidable barrier which they face. This grim opponent to faster flight is heat. Friction heat, technically known as thermodynamic heat, is the primary problem. When friction heat builds up to a temperature at which the aircraft's materials lose their strength, when the engine and the instruments cease to function properly and the man inside reaches the limits of his own endurance, the thermal barrier has been reached. In terms of today's high-speed aircraft, this condition is a frightening prospect. Most airmen are not at all sure that tomorrow's ultra-high speed aircraft will be able to fly at all without turning into a glowing ember.

Unlike the sonic wall, the heat barrier cannot be pierced; the only hope of penetrating it is to engineer a detour around it. This poses a tremendous job to the entire aircraft industry, particularly to the thermodynamicists, whose task it is to find ways of keeping both airman and airplane sufficiently cool at ever-increasing speeds.

From *Survival in the Sky* by Charles Coombs. © 1956 by Charles Coombs. By permission of William Morrow & Co., Inc. Pp. 116–17.

The removed barrier—
The unremoved barrier—
Check your answer with the key.

SELECTION 4

Purpose: To locate specific details as rapidly as possible.

Procedure: Read or skim the selection to locate as quickly as possible the answer to the following questions: "Which boys won the race?" "What was their reward?"

(117 words)

The Boat Race

THERE WAS a long blast of the siren which brought the traders and merchants of Lambarene to the landing for the cargo they were expecting. The boat had scarcely landed, when a long narrow canoe came shooting around its sides so fast a white man at the stern had just time to throw himself backward to keep from hitting the boat's cable. But the black boys rowing kept up the merry song they had been singing to the rhythm of the paddle strokes. These were the boys of the mission school with their teacher, racing a group of older boys of the mission, who came paddling up later. Because the younger boys had won, they were allowed to take the doctor and his wife in their canoe to the mission site, an hour's journey farther upstream. And the older boys followed with the luggage.

From the book *All Men Are Brothers* by Charlie May Simon. Copyright, ©, 1956 by E. P. Dutton & Co., Inc. Reprinted by permission of the publishers. P. 91.

Which boys won?—
What was the reward?—

Check your answers with the key.

Key to Selections 3 and 4—Specific Details

Selection 3—High Speed Flight
Removed barrier—Sound barrier
Unremoved barrier—Heat barrier

Selection 4—The Boat Race
Winners—The younger boys.
Reward—To take doctor and wife in canoe to mission site.

RECALLING DETAILS IN LOGICAL SEQUENCE

THE third purpose for reading (listed on page 31) is to obtain an over-all understanding of the whole article so that it can be recalled with some degree of success.

Read the following selections rapidly with the purpose in mind of understanding the material so that you can recall the main points in logical sequence. In the space provided, outline the main points in the order they are presented in the material.

SELECTION 5

Purpose: To obtain an over-all understanding of the selection so it can be recalled with success.

Procedure: Read the selection rapidly, but carefully. Note the important details and be able to recall them in logical sequence.

(135 words)

The New Empire

THE GENERATION that came to maturity between the Peace of Paris and the inauguration of President Washington had to solve more serious and original political problems than any later generation of Americans. It was then that the great beacons of American principles, such as the Declaration of Independence, the Virginia Bill of Rights, and the Federal Constitution were lighted; it was then that institutions of permanent and profound import in the history of America and of liberty were crystallized. The period was not only revolutionary and destructive, but creative and constructive; moreover the British connection was not the most important thing that was destroyed, nor was national independence the most important thing that was created. A new federal empire was erected on the ruins of the old empire, American ideas proclaimed, and the American character defined.

Samuel Eliot Morison and Henry Steele Commager. *The Growth of the American Republic,* 4th ed. Copyright 1950 by Oxford University Press, Inc. P. 128.

Write the important details from *The New Empire* in logical sequence. Check your details with those on page 35.

_____

_____

_____

_____

_____

_____

_____

_____

_____

_____

_____

_____

_____

_____

SELECTION 6

Purpose: To obtain an over-all understanding of the selection so it can be recalled with success.

Procedure: Read the selection rapidly, but carefully. Note the important details and be able to recall them in logical sequence.

(208 words)

Heat from Friction

THE PRACTICE of making fire by friction is familiar to nearly everyone. It is done simply by rubbing two pieces of wood together, usually turning a hardwood spindle in a slightly softer block. It doesn't require much spinning to generate a smoking heat. The harder the pressure and the faster the

From *Survival in the Sky* by Charles Coombs. © 1956 by Charles Coombs. By permission of William Morrow & Co., Inc. Pp. 117–18.

motion of the spindle, the more quickly first smoke and then fire results.

There are innumerable everyday illustrations of friction heat. The friction of a skidding tire against the pavement makes its own smoke. Friction created by drilling a hole in wood or metal makes the drill too hot to touch. We warm our hands on a cold day by rubbing them together. When two material substances are rubbed vigorously against each other, heat is always generated.

The air around us is definitely a material substance. Although it is an invisible, tasteless, and odorless mixture of gases, air is nevertheless a real and substantial form of matter. When any other material thing —an airplane, for instance—passes through it, thus rubbing against it, friction heat is generated. Until recently, this was no problem to aviation. At slower, subsonic speeds, the air did not offer enough resistance to the aircraft to cause undue friction. There was no dangerous heat, although airplanes in flight always heat up to some degree.

Write the important details from *Heat from Friction* in logical sequence. Check your details with those in the next column.

_____

_____

_____

_____

_____

_____

_____

_____

_____

_____

_____

_____

Key to Selections 5 and 6—Logical Sequence

Selection 5—*The New Empire*
1. Serious problems faced by people living after the Peace of Paris.
2. Beacons of American principles lighted
   —Declaration of Independence
   —Virginia Bill of Rights
   —Federal Constitution
3. Important American institution crystallized.
4. Period revolutionary—destructive then constructive.
5. New Empire erected.
6. American ideas proclaimed.
7. American character defined.

Selection 6—*Heat from Friction*
1. Fire by friction well known.
2. Rubbing two pieces of wood together creates heat.
3. Other illustrations of friction:
   —skidding tire
   —drilling a hole
   —rubbing hands together
4. Two materials rubbed together generate heat.
5. Air is a material substance. Heat therefore is generated when anything rubs against it.
6. Heat is no problem at subsonic speeds. Heat problem arises with supersonic speeds.

RECALLING DETAILS IN LOGICAL SEQUENCE— SUMMARY

As YOU worked through this third purpose for reading, that of recalling the important details in an orderly sequence, you probably found it to be a slightly more difficult task than recalling *one* main idea or searching for a specific fact.

The flexible reader adjusts himself to his purpose for reading not only in terms of speed but also in the kind and quantity of details he must locate. Development of the ability to select the main idea and important details, however, is a natural step in preparation for the difficult task of recalling items in sequence.

CRITICAL READING

THE FOURTH purpose for reading is to analyze material carefully in order to determine the author's slant, purpose, the facts presented, and so forth, and how they agree with or differ from what you already know or think about the subject.

Keeping this purpose in mind, read each of the following selections as rapidly as possible to determine the author's point of view concerning the subject. After reading each selection, summarize in several sentences, in the space provided, the author's point of view and your reaction to this viewpoint.

SELECTION 7

Purpose: To determine the author's point of view.
Procedure: Read to ascertain the author's point of view. Be ready to react to it.

(104 words)

The Great Man

WHAT I must do is all that concerns me, not what the people think. This rule, equally arduous in actual and in intellectual life, may serve for the whole distinction between greatness and meanness. It is the harder because you will always find those who think they know what is your duty better than you know it. It is easy in the world to live after the world's opinion; it is easy in soli-

tude to live after our own; but the great man is he who in the midst of the crowd keeps with perfect sweetness the independence of solitude.

A. After reading Selection 7, check the statement below which best expresses the author's belief.
   1. When we live with other people we must do what they want.
   2. It is easy to do as you wish if you live alone.
   3. It is best to live with others while doing as you wish.
B. Do you agree with the author?
   Yes ___ No ___
C. In the space below, indicate why you believe as you do.

_____

_____

_____

_____

_____

_____

_____

_____

_____

_____

_____

_____

_____

_____

_____

_____

_____

Ralph Waldo Emerson. From *The Oxford Anthology of American Literature.* Copyright 1938 by Oxford University Press, Inc. P. 464.

SELECTION 8

Purpose: To determine the author's point of view.
Procedure: Read to ascertain the author's point of view. Be ready to react to it.

(212 words)

The Secret Meeting

FREQUENTLY GROUPS of citizens seek to impose secrecy upon gatherings of private individuals called to discuss public measures. To what extent do these groups have a right to withhold from the public information of their proceedings? This is a particularly interesting question when the gatherings involved are without any legal status or are of undoubted private character.

The public's right to know seems on solid ground where the organization involved is a quasi-public agency, even though it has only an informal or social connection with public institutions. A parent-teacher association, for example, is a private association of citizens and parents and teachers. It has, however, a certain public status. When it debates the policy of a school district it becomes, in fact, a part of the government apparatus of the district, even though the relationship is not set forth in the law and the actions taken have no formal legal effect. When such groups meet to plan community actions that will result in the expenditure of public funds, the raising of public taxes, or the alteration of public policy, they move into an area in which the people have a right to know. Citizens not present have a right to know how and why recommendations were reached.

James Russell Wiggins. *Freedom or Secrecy.* Copyright 1956 by Oxford University Press, Inc. P. 22.

A. After reading Selection 8, check the statement below which best expresses the author's belief.
   1. P.T.A. meetings have no legal basis.
   2. Citizens have a right to know details of any public meeting that concerns them.
   3. When a group meets without legal status they can hold their discussions in secret.
B. Do you agree with the author? Yes ___ No ___
C. In the space below indicate why you believe as you do.

_____

Key to Selections 7 & 8—Critical Reading

A. Item 2

VOCABULARY EXERCISE I—*Selections 1–8*

Vocabulary Pre-Test has given you a chance to evaluate your knowledge of the words of our language. The various exercises presented below will help you to extend your knowledge of prefixes, suffixes, and roots. Certain exercises concern synonyms and antonyms and will demand an understanding of the meanings of the words you have read in Selections 1 through 8.

Prefixes

Underline the prefix in each of the following words. Define each prefix and write other words that contain the same prefix. The first word is completed for you.

Word	*Meaning*	*Other Words*
inexpensive	not	incapable, inactive, incompatible
thermodynamics		
quasi-public		
ultra-high		

Suffixes

Underline the suffix in each of the following words. Define each suffix and write other words containing the same suffix. The first word is completed for you.

Word	*Meaning*	*Other words*
humanity	condition or quality of being	cordiality, activity, sincerity
assortment		
turbulence		
formidable		
engineer		

Roots

Underline the root in each of the following words. Write the source word from which the root was derived (Latin, Greek, or other source) and its meaning. Then write several other words which have the same root. The first word is completed for you.

Word	*Source word*	*Meaning*	*Other words*
subsonic	sonus (L)	sound	sonant, soniferous, sonometer
constructive			
innumerable			
independence			
public			
community			
creative			

Synonyms

For each of the words listed below find other words that have the same or nearly the same meaning. If you wish to see the word used in context, make use of the selection and paragraph numbers indicated. For example, *swarmed* is in Selection 1, paragraph 1.

Word	Selection	Paragraph	Synonyms
swarmed	1	1	_____
aroma	1	1	_____
serene	2	1	_____
solitude	7	1	_____

Antonyms

For each of the words listed below find other words that have the opposite meaning. If you wish to see the word used in context, make use of the selection and paragraph numbers indicated.

Word	Selection	Paragraph	Antonyms
erected	5	1	_____
constructive	5	1	_____
greatness	7	1	_____
permanent	5	1	_____
private	8	1	_____

For your information

There are fifteen prefixes which appear most frequently in the words of our language. It will help you to know them and their meanings.

1.	ab	from		9.	in	into
2.	ad	to		10.	in	not
3.	be	by		11.	pre	before
4.	com	with		12.	pro	in front of
5.	de	from		13.	re	back
6.	dis	apart		14.	sub	under
7.	en	in		15.	un	not
8.	ex	out				

Difficulty Level of Material

THE SECOND problem in developing efficient reading is assessing the difficulty level of material.

The difficulty level can be determined rather quickly by noting the following characteristics of the material:

1. The familiarity of the topic.
2. The length of the sentences.
3. The number of many-syllabled words.
4. The number of words that are unfamiliar to you.

As an illustration and exercise in the measurement of the reading difficulty level of material, look over the following selections and determine whether you think that for your own reading you would classify them as (1) hard, (2) average, (3) easy reading.

SELECTION 9

Purpose: To determine the difficulty level of the selection.

Procedure: Skim the material and note whether the topic is a familiar one. Note also the number of words in sentences, the multi-syllabic words in the first two paragraphs (100 words), and the unfamiliar words.

(386 words)

The Weasel

SOME OF the woods creatures are about by night instead of day. The animals who have to go out each night in search of food have a difficult time in winter. There is little plant food to be found and most of these animals eat meat. Since many of their prey are sleeping through the winter, food is scarce.

As the shadows lengthen and dusk falls one of these hungry animals appears. A bloodthirsty weasel glides silently, stealthily, through the underbrush. It is difficult to see him in the darkness. Except for his eyes and nose and the black tip on his tail he is as white as the snow. With the coming of winter, white hairs had begun to grow in with the brown of his spring, summer and fall coat. The brown hairs began to fall out and he had a salt-and-pepper coat. Gradually it became more white than brown and by the time of the first snowfall he was pure white. In other seasons only his underparts are white.

As he scents a woods mouse trail, he pauses and sits up. His head sways to left and right as he tries to search out his prey. His eyes are keen and his power of scent is remarkable. He can hear the faintest cry of a small animal. All small animals fear him. While he hunts for mice, rats, chipmunks, squirrels, ducks, quail and other small animals, he himself is being hunted by birds of prey and by foxes and other larger animals.

The weasel is a surprisingly gentle mate.

From *A Book of Nature* by Pelagie Doane, copyright 1952 by Henry Z. Walck, Inc. Reprinted by permission. P. 34.

The father helps the mother to care for the babies and to hunt for food to take home to them. They stay mated and often live in the same den even after the young have left to make their own homes. Weasels have been known to have as many as twelve young, though usually there are from four to six. Their home may be in a hollow log or in a burrow under a rock. Until they are quite grown, the young follow the mother on hunting trips, spreading out from her path and then hurrying back to follow close behind her. With the approach of day they hump off to their den.

Now answer the following questions:
1. Was the topic familiar?   Yes __ No __
2. The average number of words per sentence was:
   / Less than 10 / 14–17 / 18–21 / / More than 21 /
3. The multi-syllabic words appeared to be:
   / Many / Some / Few /
4. Jot down unfamiliar words in the selection.

_____

_____

_____

_____

_____

_____

_____

5. How would you rank this selection in respect to difficulty?
   / Easy / Average / Hard /

SELECTION 10

Purpose: To determine the difficulty level of the selection.

Procedure: Skim the material and note whether the topic is a familiar one. Note also the number of words in sentences, the multi-syllabic words in the first two paragraphs (100 words), and the unfamiliar words.

(103 words)

The Invention

NEAR THE Sforza castle in Milan was the church and monastery of Santa Maria della Grazia. Leonardo was commissioned to paint a picture of the Last Supper for the new dining room of the monastery.

Leonardo was elated and plunged into the work feverishly. He would work far into the night and lie in bed late in the mornings, planning the painting in his mind. In order to force himself to get up, he invented a peculiar alarm clock. It was a contraption with pulleys attached to his bed which, at a certain hour in the morning, would raise his feet in the air.

From *Leonardo da Vinci* by Elizabeth Ripley. Copyright 1952 by Oxford University Press, Inc. Reprinted by permission of Henry Z. Walck, Inc. P. 22.

Now answer the following questions about Selection 10:
1. Was the topic familiar?   Yes __ No __
2. The average number of words per sentence was:
/Less than 10 / 14–17 / 18–21 / More than 21 /
3. The multi-syllabic words appeared to be:
/ Many / Some / Few /
4. Jot down unfamiliar words in the selection.

_____

_____

_____

_____

5. How would you rank this selection in respect to difficulty?
/ Easy / Average / Hard /

SELECTION 11

Purpose: To determine the difficulty level of the selection.
Procedure: Skim the material and note whether the topic is a familiar one. Note also the number of words in sentences, the multi-syllabic words in the first two paragraphs (100 words), and the unfamiliar words.

(112 words)

George Washington

A GENERATION passed before Washington's services in time of peace were adequately appreciated in his own country; and as his personality has faded into legend, it has been clothed in army uniform. Washington's unique place in history rests not only on his leadership in war, and his influence in organizing the Federal Government; not merely on his integrity, good judgment, and magnanimity, but also on his courageous stand for peace when his countrymen were clamoring to embark on an unnecessary war. This quiet, plain-speaking gentleman of Virginia glimpsed a truth hidden from his more talented contemporaries: that the means by which a nation advances, especially in its adolescence, are as important as the ends which it pursues.

Samuel Eliot Morison and Henry Steele Commager. *The Growth of the American Republic,* 4th ed. Copyright 1950 by Oxford University Press, Inc. P. 369.

Now answer the following questions about Selection 11:
1. Was the topic familiar?   Yes __ No __
2. The average number of words per sentence was:
/Less than 10 / 14–17 / 18–21 / More than 21 /
3. The multi-syllabic words appeared to be:
/ Many / Some / Few /
4. Jot down unfamiliar words in the selection.

_____

_____

_____

_____

5. How would you rank this selection in respect to difficulty?
/ Easy / Average / Hard /

SELECTION 12

Purpose: To determine the difficulty level of the selection.

Procedure: Skim the material and note whether the topic is a familiar one. Note also the number of words in sentences, the multi-syllabic words in the selection, and the unfamiliar words.

(172 words)

Thomas Jefferson

JEFFERSON WAS not in any social sense a democrat, and only in a political sense by contrast with his contemporaries. A gentleman philosopher like many of the French noblesse, with a classical education, an exquisite taste, a lively curiosity, and a belief in the perfectibility of man, he was of the eighteenth rather than the nineteenth century. Deeply religious without being a churchman, he had the serenity of one to whom now and then the Spirit has not disdained to speak. The extraordinary ascendancy that he enjoyed in the hearts of the masses was attained without speech-making, military service, or catering to vulgar prejudices. The secret of Jefferson's power lay in the fact that he appealed to and expressed

Samuel Eliot Morison and Henry Steele Commager. *The Growth of the American Republic*, 4th ed. Copyright 1950 by Oxford University Press, Inc. Pp. 382–3.

America's better self: her idealism, simplicity, youthful mind, and hopeful outlook, rather than those material, practical, and selfish qualities on which Hamilton based his policy. Jefferson's political object was to prove that people circumstanced like the Americans were ripe for "a government founded not on the fears and follies of man, but on his reason, on the predominance of his social over his dissocial passions."

Now answer the following questions about Selection 12:

1. Was the topic familiar?   Yes __ No __
2. The average number of words per sentence was:
   /Less than 10 / 14–17 / 18–21 / More than 21 /
3. The multi-syllabic words appeared to be:
   / Many / Some / Few /
4. Jot down unfamiliar words in the selection.

   _____

   _____

   _____

   _____

   _____

5. How would you rank this selection in respect to difficulty?
   / Easy / Average / Hard /

VOCABULARY EXERCISE II—*Selections 9–12*

Prefixes

Underline the prefix in each of the following words. Define each prefix and write other words that contain the same prefix.

Word	*Meaning*	*Other words*
retrace	_____	_____
advance	_____	_____
unnecessary	_____	_____
predominance	_____	_____
expel	_____	_____

Suffixes

Underline the suffix in each of the following words. Define each suffix and write other words containing the same suffix.

Word	Meaning	Other words
silently	_____	_____
darkness	_____	_____
faintest	_____	_____
generation	_____	_____
courageous	_____	_____

Roots

Underline the root of each of the following words. Write the source word from which the root was derived (Latin, Greek, or other source) and its meaning. Then write several other words that have the same root.

Word	Source word	Meaning	Other words
personality	_____	_____	_____
contemporaries	_____	_____	_____
democrat	_____	_____	_____
philosopher	_____	_____	_____
object	_____	_____	_____

Synonyms

For each of the words listed below find other words that have the same or nearly the same meaning. If you wish to see the word used in context, make use of the selection and paragraph numbers indicated.

Word	Selection	Paragraph	Synonyms
prey	9	1	_____
stealthily	9	2	_____
legend	11	1	_____
talented	11	1	_____
masses	12	1	_____

Antonyms

For each of the words listed below find other words that have the opposite meaning. If you wish to see the word used in context, make use of the selection and paragraph numbers indicated.

Word	Selection	Paragraph	Antonyms
unique	11	1	_____
gentle	9	4	_____
extraordinary	12	1	_____
vulgar	12	1	_____
social	12	1	_____

For your information

Many English words are derived from Latin. We suggest that the following Latin roots, their meaning, and the stem found in English derivatives be studied.

Latin root	Meaning	Stem
annus	year	ann, enn
aqua	water	aqua
audire	to hear	aud
caput	head	cap
cedere	to go, to move	ced, cess
centum	one hundred	cent
dicere	to say or tell	dic
ducere	to take or lead	duc
fortis	strong	fort
gratus	pleasing	grat
mittere	to let go or to send	mit
pars	a part	part
pellere	to drive	pel
portare	to carry	port
scribere	to write	scrib
tempus	time	tempor
videre	to see	vid, vis
vivere	to live	viv

Familiarity

THE THIRD factor affecting efficient reading is the degree of familiarity possessed by a person with the subject under consideration. We all know a little about many things. Some people have a great deal of information on many subjects. But even for these fortunate individuals there are some subjects they are less familiar with than others. Most of us know a great deal about a few things and relatively little about many things.

The research of the authors has shown that in order for a person to read a piece of printed material with a high level of understanding he must already be familiar with or must know approximately 90 per cent of the basic ideas presented in that material. In other words, the ease, speed, efficiency, and level of understanding with which a person can read any given written material depend to a great extent upon how much he already knows about the subject being discussed.

This may be illustrated, first by reading sections in an elementary textbook in any specific subject such as biology, for example, and then by reading sections in an advanced text written on the same subject. The reader will find not only the vocabulary and sentence structure much more difficult in the advanced text, but also, unless he has a good background in or familiarity with the subject, that it requires slower reading, more careful concentration, and more thinking in order to understand the advanced text material.

When he reads, an efficient reader is actually searching for ideas or information that are new to him. It is seldom an efficient use of reading time to read material slowly and carefully if it concerns a subject about which you already know a great deal. You can skim such material rapidly in order to refresh your memory or to search for any new bits of information or ideas the author might be presenting.

Thus, the more familiar you are with the subject and ideas in a given piece of printed material, the more rapidly you should be able to read that material with a high level of understanding. Conversely, the less familiar you are with the subject or ideas about which you are reading, the more slowly and carefully you will have to read in order to attain the same level of understanding.

Following is a familiarity index which may be used as a guide in assessing your familiarity with the material in the exercises included in this section, and to other materials you may encounter in your daily reading.

1. *High degree of familiarity*—The subject is in my field of special interest and study. I read about it and deal with the ideas involved almost daily.
2. *Slightly above average familiarity*—I studied this in high school, but have not read or thought about it much since. I am not especially interested in the subject.
3. *Average degree of familiarity*—I heard a program or discussion concerning this recently and was interested in it, but am familiar with only the generalities of the subject.
4. *Slightly below average familiarity*—I have heard this discussed or "batted around," but was not particularly interested and know little about it.
5. *No knowledge*—I have no knowledge of this subject at all.

Determining your familiarity calls for a rapid skimming of the material to see what it is about, which involves (1) a check of the title, (2) noting author's name or the source, (3) a glance through the material to see whether or not it is a topic with which you are already familiar, (4) a look at the last paragraph or two to pick up the author's summary of what he has written.

Try this with the following selection, which has been set up as a sample of how this might work for you. Then, using this same procedure, glance quickly through the next selections and indicate, in the space provided, where on the familiarity scale they fall.

SELECTION 13

Purpose: To determine your degree of familiarity with the material.

Procedure: Using the skimming technique, follow the marginal notes to determine your degree of familiarity with the following selection. When you have finished, check the familiarity scale found at the end of the selection.

(252 words)

A Doctor's Reward

BY CHARLIE MAY SIMON

√ (Title)
√ (Author)
√ (Lead sentence of paragraph)

A DOCTOR needs to conserve his emotional strength and energy, so he can give the same attention to all. But try as he would, Dr. Schweitzer could not put from his mind the immense pity and anxiety he felt for each patient. He suffered with them in their pain and weakness. To him it had been well worth any amount of sacrifice or discomfort, well worth all the years of study and preparation to come here, just to see the joy of those who had been plagued with sores, after they had been cleanly bandaged so they no longer had to drag their poor bleeding feet through the mud. And sweeter than any music was the contented cooing of a baby that had been crying in pain.

Akewa the word that meant "thank you," √ was often heard. Many wanted to show their gratitude by bringing gifts, or offering what little money they could afford. One payment that meant a great deal was labor done for the hospital. An uncle of a boy that had been brought in covered with sores spent fourteen days making cupboards for the hospital out of packing boxes. A black trader offered the services of his workers,

From the book *All Men Are Brothers* by Charlie May Simon. Copyright, ©, 1956 by E. P. Dutton & Co., Inc. Reprinted by permission of the publishers. Pp. 107–8.

(Final paragraph usually a summary of the article)

so that the roof of the doctor's own cottage could be repaired.

The greatest reward of all came when, after an operation was over and the patient had regained consciousness, the doctor felt a hand reach out for his own and cling to it. And it was with joy he heard the words, "I've no more pain! I've no more pain!"

How do you rate the degree of familiarity you have with this topic? Check point on the familiarity scale that best describes it.

FAMILIARITY SCALE

1   2   3
/ High / Above Average / Average /
4   5
/ Below Average / No Knowledge /

SELECTION 14

Purpose: To determine your degree of familiarity with the material.
Procedure: Using the skimming technique, determine your degree of familiarity with the following selection. When you have finished, check the familiarity scale found at the end of the selection.

(153 words)

The Sea in Spring

BY RACHEL L. CARSON

IN THE sea, as on land, spring is a time for the renewal of life. During the long months of winter in the temperate zones the surface waters have been absorbing the cold. Now the heavy water begins to sink, slipping down and displacing the warmer layers below. Rich stores of minerals have been accumulating on the floor of the continental shelf—some freighted down the rivers from the lands; some derived from sea creatures

Rachel L. Carson. *The Sea Around Us*. Copyright 1950, 1951 by Rachel L. Carson. Reprinted by permission of Oxford University Press, Inc. P. 29.

that have died and whose remains have drifted down to the bottom; some from the shells that once encased a diatom, the streaming protoplasm of a radiolarian, or the transparent tissues of a pteropod. Nothing is wasted in the sea; every particle of material is used over and over again, first by one creature, then by another. And when in spring the waters are deeply stirred, the warm bottom water brings to the surface a rich supply of minerals, ready for use by new forms of life.

How do you rate the degree of familiarity you have with this topic? Check point on the familiarity scale that best describes it.

FAMILIARITY SCALE

1   2   3
/ High / Above Average / Average /
4   5
/ Below Average / No Knowledge /

SELECTION 15

Purpose: To determine your degree of familiarity with the material.
Procedure: Using the skimming technique, determine your degree of familiarity with the following selection. When you have finished, check the familiarity scale found at the end of the selection.

(192 words)

Helicopters

BY CHARLES COOMBS

EVERYONE IS familiar with the hovering helicopters, which have become such an important part of both military and civilian flying. Their importance increases daily.

From *Survival in the Sky* by Charles Coombs. © 1956 by Charles Coombs. By permission of William Morrow & Co., Inc. Pp. 236–8.

Despite their apparent clumsiness, they are without equal in rescue operations, or in transporting men and supplies over short distances and in and out of areas where no airfields are available. Although vulnerable to attack, they are less so than trucks or lorries or other ground-crawling military vehicles.

In civilian use, the helicopter's ability to land on a dime makes it exceptionally valuable for short hops and for shuttle service in and out of crowded areas. Always hovering on their horizontally spinning rotors, the choppers are not able to travel at much over 100 miles per hour. Yet since flying eliminates traffic delays on busy thoroughfares, helicopters are tremendously useful for short-distance travel. Their ability to make spot landings and take-offs is also a convenience. In the coming years the use of helicopters is certain to increase enormously. They will be used as cargo carriers, passenger carriers, and even as personal pleasure and business craft. Many a garage will be occupied by both an automobile and a small family "whirlybird."

How do you rate the degree of familiarity you have with this topic? Check point on the familiarity scale that best describes it.

FAMILIARITY SCALE

1	2	3
/ High /	Above Average /	Average /

4	5
/ Below Average /	No Knowledge /

SELECTION 16

Purpose: To determine your degree of familiarity with the material.

Procedure: Using the skimming technique, determine your degree of familiarity with the following selection. When you have finished, check the familiarity scale found at the end of the selection.

(113 words)

Safety in Boats

BY HARRY ZARCHY

SAFETY IS a very important factor in the design and construction of any boat. Should a wooden boat capsize, it will float. Boats made of non-floating materials will sink. Manufacturers solve this problem in a variety of ways. Canvas boats may have inflated sections, forming floating pockets. Metal boats usually have sealed flotation tanks built into the hull at some point. Plastic boats frequently use blocks of Styrofoam, an extremely light material that will keep the boat afloat; sometimes air chambers are built into the hull. The important thing is to keep the boat from sinking if it turns over, and every boat builder has worked out a solution to the problem.

Harry Zarchy. *Let's Go Boating.* Copyright 1952 by Alfred A. Knopf, Inc. Pp. 7–8.

How do you rate the degree of familiarity you have with this topic? Check point on the familiarity scale that best describes it.

FAMILIARITY SCALE

1	2	3
/ High /	Above Average /	Average /

4	5
/ Below Average /	No Knowledge /

FAMILIARITY—SUMMARY

LET US consider what the familiarity rating means to you as a reader. If you rated one of the selections "1"—High Familiarity— it means that in all probability you already know about 90 per cent of the material. About 10 per cent of the ideas presented will be new—and the chances are that these are merely new applications or interpretations or "angles" to which the ideas you already know can be applied.

This means that you should be able to cover such material extremely rapidly since you will not be confronted by problems of vocabulary or understanding. You will be able to skim over the material you already know, merely verifying your present knowledge; you should read more slowly the few portions containing new ideas. Your speed will be governed in this case largely by the purpose you have set for reading the material.

If your familiarity with the subject is average your approach will take the form of careful reading, again depending upon your purpose for reading and the level of difficulty of the material.

If you have assessed the material you read as "5"—No Knowledge—you will in all probability find it necessary to approach the article with a study-type method of reading. In this case you will undoubtedly find many new ideas and will as a result find reading the material difficult. In fact there is a good possibility that if you have no prior knowledge of a subject you will find yourself able to read only the most elementary discussions of that subject if you are to understand what you read.

VOCABULARY EXERCISE III—*Selections 13–16*

Prefixes
Underline the prefix in each of the following words. Define each prefix and write other words containing the same prefixes.

Word	Meaning	Other words
immense		
discomfort		
absorbing		
encased		
automobile		

Suffixes
Underline the suffix in each of the following words. Define each suffix and write other words containing the same suffix.

Word	Meaning	Other words
continental		
plastic		
temperate		
greatest		
importance		

Roots
Underline the root of each of the following words. Write the source word from which the root was derived and its meaning. Then write other words which have the same root.

Word	Source word	Meaning	Other words
gratitude			
temperate			

Word	Source word	Meaning	Other words
protoplasm	———————	———————	———————
helicopters	———————	———————	———————
manufacturers	———————	———————	———————

Synonyms

For each of the words listed below find other words which have the same or nearly the same meaning. If you wish to see the word used in context, make use of the selection and paragraph numbers indicated.

Word	Selection	Paragraph	Synonyms
patient	13	3	———————————
plagued	13	1	———————————
particle	14	1	———————————
vulnerable	15	1	———————————
solve	16	1	———————————

Antonyms

For each of the words listed below find other words which have the opposite meaning. If you wish to see the word used in context, make use of the selection and paragraph numbers indicated.

Word	Selection	Paragraph	Antonyms
transparent	14	1	———————————
clumsiness	15	1	———————————
horizontally	15	2	———————————
discomfort	13	1	———————————
regained	13	3	———————————

For your information

Many English words are derived from Greek. We suggest that the following Greek roots, their meaning, and the stem found in English derivatives be studied.

Greek root	Meaning	Stem
autos	self	auto
biblion	book	biblio
bios	life	bio
cosmos	would	cosmo
demos	people	demo
graphein	to write	graph
logos	word or speech	log
metron	measure	metr
phone	sound	phon
tele	far	tele

PRACTICING EFFICIENT READING

YOU HAVE learned that flexibility is a most important key to efficient reading. You now know that flexibility may be obtained through the use of three techniques:

1. Identifying your *purpose* for reading.
2. Assessing the *difficulty level* of the reading material.
3. Deciding your *familiarity* with a topic.

In the following selections you are asked to apply all three of these techniques in order to demonstrate your improved approach to reading materials.

Before reading each selection consider the three preceding statements. Then read the selection and fill in the questions at the end.

SELECTION 17

Purpose: To read and apply the three techniques you have studied in order to improve your reading flexibility.

Your Task: 1. To determine the *main idea* of the selection.

2. To determine the *difficulty level* of the selection.

3. To determine your *familiarity* with the topic of the selection.

Procedure: Read the selection that follows as quickly as you can and then be ready to react to the three tasks listed above.

(313 words)

Rocks

ROCK IS the commonest thing in the world.

Who has not picked up a stone and flung it high in the air? Who has not made a pebble skip over the water? We do these things just as naturally as we breathe. We are so used to handling stones and stepping on them and kicking them with our feet, it

Anne Terry White. *All About Our Changing Rocks.* Copyright 1955 by Anne Terry White. Reprinted by permission of Random House, Inc. Pp. 1–2.

never occurs to us that rock is the most valuable thing there is.

But isn't that a contradiction—the commonest and the most valuable?

Maybe it sounds that way. But there is no contradiction in it. For nearly everything that makes life possible came out of the rocks.

Much of our air came out of the rocks. Much of our water came out of the rocks and all of our soil did. We often hear someone say of a thing, "It's cheap as dirt." But dirt isn't cheap. We found that out when the wind blew away the top soil of Oklahoma and turned rich farms into wasteland. Everything that lives on land owes its life to the soil, and the soil is rock that has decayed. Neither plants nor animals nor we ourselves would be here if it were not for rock.

Do you doubt the value of rock? Look around. You will be startled by the list of common things made of rock or some product of the rock. In five minutes you will count a hundred.

Here is a stone building, a wall, a foundation, stone window trim and steps, a monument, a pier, a bridge, a breakwater. Here are asphalt sidewalks, cement pavements, gravel walks, bricks, curbstones and windowpanes. The mirror over the dresser is a product of the rock. So is the glass from which we drink. So are the dishes on the table. Yes, even the pots, pans, spoons and knives.

For metal, too, comes out of the rocks.

1. What is the main idea of this selection?

_____

_____

2. Reading difficulty—How difficult do you consider this selection?

/ Unusually Hard / Hard / Average /
/ Easy / Unusually Easy /

3. Familiarity—How familiar are you with the topic discussed in this selection?

    1   2   3
/ High / Above Average / Average /
    4   5
/ Below Average / No Knowledge /

SELECTION 18

Purpose: To read and apply the three techniques you have studied in order to improve your reading flexibility.

Your Task: 1. To determine the *main idea* of the selection.

2. To determine the *difficulty level* of the selection.

3. To determine your *familiarity* with the topic of the selection.

Procedure: Read the selection that follows as quickly as you can and then be ready to react to the three tasks listed above.

(368 words)

Man and Mechanisms

WITH MOST of his work taken from him, the airman simply sits in the cockpit and maintains a visual check on his flight instruments. The electronically controlled craft continues to track its quarry and, at the correct instant, automatically fires its guns or rockets, or both. Some of the rockets have their own electronic minds, too, and home in on their target with pinpoint accuracy.

With his mission accomplished, the pilot may choose to take over and fly back home; or he may allow his automatic control system to find the way back to the base, and even take him in for a landing. As one pilot said, "Those electronic gadgets will do everything but tuck you in bed."

So we are faced with the question: what is the pilot doing in the airplane anyway? If everything can be handled automatically by electronics, why have a man taking up room and adding weight?

From *Survival in the Sky* by Charles Coombs. © 1956 by Charles Coombs. By permission of William Morrow & Co., Inc. Pp. 206–9.

The reason is largely that electronic machines have no flexibility. They are fed certain information through electrical impulses, which dictate the machine's action with mathematical precision. Feed the same information, and the machine will always come up with the same reaction. But there are times when a slight error may occur. Then, unless some kind of human judgment is available, great havoc may result. Without judgment or flexibility, an electronic machine can become an unwitting robot of destruction. Only man has these essential characteristics, and they can make a big and important difference.

One is reminded of the story of Colonel Charles Lindbergh, who was flying a bombing and strafing mission over a small South Pacific island in enemy hands during World War II. He set his plane on its diving course and sighted in on a distant building far below. As he roared down upon his target, he held his thumb on the bomb-release button, ready to drop his cargo of destruction. Suddenly a small cross loomed in his bombsight. He took his finger off the button. As he zoomed away from the tops of the coconut palms, he saw plainly that the target he had unwittingly chosen was a church. Shaken by the thought of what he had almost done, the famous flyer flew on with his bombs still racked beneath his wings. An electronic control and firepower system would not have heeded that cross!

1. What is the main idea of this selection?

_____

_____

2. Reading difficulty—How difficult do you consider this selection?

/ Unusually Hard / Hard / Average /
/ Easy / Unusually Easy /

3. Familiarity—How familiar are you with the topic discussed in this selection?

    1   2   3
/ High / Above Average / Average /
    4   5
/ Below Average / No Knowledge /

SELECTION 19

Purpose: To read and apply the three techniques you have studied in order to improve your reading flexibility.

Your Task: 1. To determine the *main idea* of the selection.

2. To determine the *difficulty level* of the selection.

3. To determine your *familiarity* with the topic of the selection.

Procedure: Read the selection that follows as quickly as you can and then be ready to react to the three tasks listed above.

(252 words)

The Ills of the Ignorant

DR. SCHWEITZER realized the small differences between the customs and practices of one race and another should not be taken too seriously. He noticed that mothers of newborn babies had themselves and their children painted white all over, to make them look terrifying to the evil spirits. He could even tease, and with a twinkle in his eye he would remind them, as soon as the baby was born, to take care they didn't forget the paint.

Dr. Schweitzer saw how these people were pitiful victims of their fears and superstitions, as well as of disease. The gods they worshiped were evil gods. They had no prayers of praise or love or thanks. Their prayers were only offerings and deprecation. They lived in constant dread of some voodoo or evil spell that might be cast upon them, or some taboo, which if broken would surely bring death. Disease itself, they thought, did not happen from any natural cause, but through some evil spirit or a spell cast on them by some human enemy. A worm somehow had been put inside their bodies to eat away the part affected.

From the book *All Men Are Brothers* by Charlie May Simon. Copyright, ©, 1956 by E. P. Dutton & Co., Inc. Reprinted by permission of the publishers. Pp. 102–3.

"The worm is eating in my stomach," one with stomach pains would say, in describing the symptoms.

The medicine that cured them was a magic charm to make the worm crawl away.

To the doctor, it seemed that there was as great a need to free the minds of these people from their fears and taboos as there was to heal their bodies. He saw many a poor, frightened creature, so dominated by a belief in some taboo that he died of nothing more than a physical and mental shock, because the taboo was broken.

1. What is the main idea of this selection?

_____

_____

_____

2. Reading difficulty—How difficult do you consider this selection?

/ Unusually Hard / Hard / Average /
/ Easy / Unusually Easy /

3. Familiarity—How familiar are you with the topic discussed in this selection?
    1   2   3
/ High / Above Average / Average /
    4   5
/ Below Average / No Knowledge /

SELECTION 20

Purpose: To read and apply the three techniques you have studied in order to improve your reading efficiency.

Your Task: 1. To determine the *main idea* of each paragraph in this selection.

2. To determine the *difficulty level* of the selection.

3. To determine your *familiarity* with the topic of the selection.

Procedure: Read the selection that follows as quickly as you can and then be ready to react to the three tasks listed above. Underline one important statement in each paragraph.

(419 words)

Bees

IN THE spring the bees visit the maple trees to gather the pollen and the nectar and take it to their hive in the hollow of an old tree. There are many layers of cells in the hive. In some the food is stored. In some the eggs are laid. There is only one queen bee in a hive, even though fifty thousand bees may live there. The queen lays the eggs, as many as six a minute. The drones, or males, fertilize some of the eggs. These drones come from fertilized eggs. Tens of thousands of bees come from unfertilized eggs. These are the workers. They build the hive, gather food, keep the house tidy and tend the newborn.

When the baby bee, or grub, emerges from the egg it is blind and helpless. It has no wings or feet. It has no feelers. It is mostly all stomach. The worker-nurses feed it for the first two days on royal jelly, for the next three days on honey and pollen. If the nurses find a baby bee in a queen bee cell they do not change its diet, but continue to feed it royal jelly. This bee will grow up to be a queen bee. After five days, the bee has grown fifteen hundred times larger than when it emerged from the egg.

Now it is ready to spin its cocoon. In the cocoon changes take place. In about three weeks a bee emerges from the cocoon. If the bee is a worker it begins to work immediately and throughout its life goes from one task to another. Perhaps this is why they do not live very long. Some of the drones live longer. They live until cold weather comes. The queen bee lives longest—sometimes as long as four to six years. The first task of the worker is to help take care of the baby bees and to feed them royal jelly and bee bread and honey. Bee bread is made from the pollen of flowers. When the worker is six days old she starts making royal jelly by means of glands in her head.

From *A Book of Nature* by Pelagie Doane, copyright 1952 by Henry Z. Walck, Inc. Reprinted by permission. Pp. 6–7.

When the worker is two weeks old she tries her wings. She leaves the darkness of her home for the bright sunshine near its entrance. Before she is ready to go out in the meadow to gather pollen and nectar, there is another task she must attend to— she must make wax which the builders of the hive will use to repair and enlarge the home. Then she is ready to join her sisters who are gathering pollen and nectar from the flowers in the meadow. The bees hum from flower to flower in the meadow, sipping from clovers and dandelions and violets, daisies and other flowers.

1. Write out the main idea of each paragraph in this selection.

_____

_____

_____

_____

_____

_____

_____

_____

_____

_____

_____

_____

2. Reading difficulty—How difficult do you consider this selection?
   / Unusually Hard / Hard / Average /
   / Easy / Unusually Easy /

3. Familiarity—How familiar are you with the topic discussed in this selection?

   1   2   3
   / High / Above Average / Average /
   4   5
   / Below Average / No Knowledge /

VOCABULARY EXERCISE IV—*Selections 17–20*

Prefixes

Underline the prefix in each of the following words. Define each prefix and write other words containing the same prefix.

Word	*Meaning*	*Other words*
contradiction		
affected		
superstitions		
unwittingly		

Suffixes

Underline the suffix in each of the following words. Define each suffix and write other words containing the same suffix.

Word	*Meaning*	*Other words*
pavement		
accuracy		
flexibility		
fertilize		
helpless		

Roots

Underline the root of each of the following words. Write the source word from which the root was derived and its meaning. Then write other words that have the same root.

Word	*Source word*	*Meaning*	*Other words*
product			
asphalt			
electronics			
deprecations			
dominated			

Synonyms

For each of the words listed below find other words which have the same or nearly the same meaning. If you wish to see the word used in context, make use of the selection and paragraph numbers indicated.

Word	*Selection*	*Paragraph*	*Synonyms*
pebble	17	2	
pier	17	7	
havoc	18	4	

Word	Selection	Paragraph	Synonyms
zoomed	18	5	_____
taboo	19	2	_____
hum	20	4	_____

Antonyms

For each of the words listed below find other words which have the opposite meaning. If you wish to see the word used in context, make use of the selection and paragraph numbers indicated.

Word	Selection	Paragraph	Antonyms
cheap	17	5	_____
quarry	18	1	_____
enlarge	20	4	_____
symptoms	19	3	_____
controlled	18	1	_____

For your information

There are many suffixes in the English language. We have listed twenty-eight of the most common suffixes and their meanings. If you can learn these you will be aided greatly in your mastery of vocabulary.

1. able—having the quality or capacity
2. al—having the character of
3. ance—action or process
4. ant—one who
5. ary—pertaining to
6. ation—act or doing, state of being
7. ee—one to whom an act is done
8. eer—one who is concerned with
9. ence—act or state of being
10. er—one who, process of
11. ess—female
12. ful—full of, characterized by
13. fy—to make, form into
14. ible—having the quality or fitness
15. ic—of the nature of
16. ion—act of, state of
17. ism—act of, state of, doctrine of
18. ist—one who practices given action or conduct
19. ity—state, condition, quality
20. ive—having the quality of
21. ize—to subject to, make into or like
22. less—without, beyond the range of
23. ment—state, condition, quality
24. ness—state, condition, quality
25. or—state or quality of, one who
26. ous—full of, having qualities of
27. ty—quality, state, condition
28. y—full of, inclined to

SELECTION 21

Purpose: To read and apply the three techniques you have studied in order to improve your reading efficiency.

Your Task: 1. To determine the *main idea* of each paragraph in this selection.

2. To determine the *difficulty level* of the selection.

3. To determine your *familiarity* with the topic of the selection.

Procedure: Read the selection that follows as quickly as you can and then be ready to react to the three tasks listed above. Underline one important statement in each paragraph.

(384 words)

Gravity

GRAVITY—OR its absence—is a basic factor in man's survival and ability to function. Since supersonic aviation tends to disturb the balance of gravity in a startling fashion, this area of research is of major importance to future flight.

Gravitation is a master principle governing the universe. Having always lived with gravity, most of us accept its existence without even a shrug. If gravity is what holds us to the ground, fine. If the entire universe is governed by its force, and this force is not likely to be shut off, why worry about it? Hence, for centuries no one gave gravity any particular thought. In fact, no one even bothered to give it a label until the latter part of the seventeenth century, when a thoughtful philosopher and mathematican named Isaac Newton took the time and effort to figure it out. By watching an apple fall from a tree, he concluded that if there were no ground beneath the tree to stop the apple, it would continue falling all the way to the center of the earth. This implies that if the ground were suddenly jerked out from under any object, it would start falling

From *Survival in the Sky* by Charles Coombs. © 1956 by Charles Coombs. By permission of William Morrow & Co., Inc. Pp. 72, 74, 75, 81, 82.

toward the center of the earth, stopping only when it reached the very core. There, theoretically, the gravitational pull from all directions meets and creates a neutral zone. Newton's theory is accepted as fact, even though we cannot actually see it in operation.

It has also been determined that the speed of an object pulled downward by gravity increases at the rate of 32.2 feet per second. This means that the object would build up an amazing speed in a very short period of time. For example, within a minute and a half, the object would be falling at a rate of nearly 3000 feet per second, or approximately 2000 miles per hour.

The surface of the earth itself offers the most resistance to gravity. Gravity's constant downward pull is opposed by the constant upward push of the earth. When the upward force of resistance exactly balances the downward pull of gravity, the object affected is static, or at rest. This, of course, is the condition that exists in any motionless object.

One of the major problems of aviation research and development is to find out how much increased gravitational pull can be endured by flyers. It is essential to know this in order to determine what protection must be furnished to see them through emergencies causing exaggerated gravitational strain. The proper answers can be reached only through lengthy programs of actual testing.

1. Write down the main ideas you have underlined in each paragraph.

_____

_____

_____

_____

_____

_____

_____

_____

_____

_____

_____

_____

2. Reading difficulty—How difficult do you consider this selection?
/ Unusually Hard / Hard / Average /
/ Easy / Unusually Easy /

3. Familiarity—How familiar are you with the topic discussed in this selection?
   1   2   3
/ High / Above Average / Average /
         4   5
/ Below Average / No Knowledge /

SELECTION 22

Purpose: To read and apply the three techniques you have studied in order to improve your reading efficiency.

Your Task: 1. To determine the *main idea* of each paragraph in this selection.

2. To determine the *difficulty level* of the selection.

3. To determine your *familiarity* with the topic of the selection.

Procedure: Read the selection that follows as quickly as you can and then be ready to react to the three tasks listed above. Underline one important statement in each paragraph.

(324 words)

Albert Schweitzer— Medical Student

ON A damp foggy day near the end of October of that same year, the young medical students in the anatomy class saw a man of thirty come into the room and take

From the book *All Men Are Brothers* by Charlie May Simon. Copyright, ©, 1956 by E. P. Dutton & Co., Inc. Reprinted by permission of the publishers. Pp. 76–7.

his place as a freshman among them. He was tall and strongly built, with dark, unruly hair and the kind of heavy, bristling mustache popular with the men of the time. His hazel eyes had a way of twinkling with ready laughter and friendship, yet there was something also in their expression which set him apart from others in the room.

Some of the students might have recognized him as the professor who lectured on philosophy at the University. Others may have heard his sermons at the Church of St. Nicholas beside the river Ill, or they might have known him as the Principal of the Theological College. And those who loved music had heard him play the organ at the Bach concerts at St. William's Church near by.

But what was he doing here, they wondered. Why would he be starting as a freshman in this class on anatomy? They saw him again in the other classes, in physiology, chemistry, physics, zoology and botany, listening to the lectures and taking notes as they were doing. But why?

The students were not the only ones who asked the question. The dean of the medical school himself, the professors in the Philosophy Department and all of Albert Schweitzer's other friends were asking the same question. Why should a man who already had a doctor's degree in theology and another in philosophy, whose book, *Bach, the Musician Poet,* just published in French, was so popular there was now a demand for it in German, too, and whose essay on organs had been widely read, be coming here now as a freshman to begin the long, hard course in medicine?

It had not been an easy decision for Albert Schweitzer to make. He could look with impatience upon the stretch of years ahead, when he must prepare for the work he had undertaken. But he had thought his reasons for it would be understood. From Paris, where he had gone that summer, he had written to relatives and a few close friends, telling of his plan to begin the study of medicine so that he could give the help most needed to the people of Africa.

1. Write down the main ideas you have underlined in each paragraph.

_____

_____

_____

_____

_____

_____

_____

_____

_____

_____

2. Reading difficulty—How difficult do you consider this selection?

/ Unusually Hard / Hard / Average /
/ Easy / Unusually Easy /

3. Familiarity—How familiar are you with the topic discussed in this selection?

1	2	3

/ High / Above Average / Average /

4		5

/ Below Average / No Knowledge /

SELECTION 23

Purpose: To recall specific details in logical sequence.

Procedure: Read the selection and note the most important details as rapidly as possible. After reading the selection, refer to your notes and write in outline form, in the space provided, the most important details. Use complete sentences.

(338 words)

The Caterpillar

ON A blade of grass a fat brown-haired caterpillar is slowly eating her lunch. She

From *A Book of Nature* by Pelagie Doane, copyright 1952 by Henry Z. Walck, Inc. Reprinted by permission. P. 7.

is called a wooly bear. She slept most of the winter through. When she wakened she was shabby and thin and very hungry. She ate and she ate, until she was fat. She had nibbled the nearby grass blades until there was only lacework on the stems. She is quivering now, and wriggling out of her coat! She is nearly out of it and she is kicking it off.

Her new coat is thick. It is brown with a black band at each end. Her feet are dark red and her face is black. This is not the first time she has shed her old coat. Ever since she ate her way out of her eggshell she has been changing coats. Whenever a coat became too tight she un-zipped it and wriggled out in a coat that was bigger and prettier. This, however, is the last time she will change her coat. It is not, though, the last time she will change. She creeps along now to the underside of a dry twig. Here she hangs, back down, and begins to spin a cocoon. From her under-lip comes a silk-like thread which stiffens in the air. She weaves this thread about her body. As she weaves she pulls out hairs from her body and interlaces them in the thread. When she works on the right side she pulls the hairs from the right side. When she works on the left side she pulls the hairs from the left side. When she finishes her cocoon she has used every hair.

When she emerges from her cocoon she will no longer be a caterpillar. She will be a moth. She will be called a salt marsh moth. The upper part of her body will be white, the lower half tan with a row of black dots. She will have two white wings and two tan, and they will be dotted with black. Some moths fly at night but this moth will fly by day. Every day, until it is time for her to lay her eggs, she will fly about the meadow, visiting the flowers. When she lays her eggs there will be about two hundred laid in rows.

In the space provided, list the important details you noted.

denly the stick starts twisting and turning in his hands. Then he announces that there is water under that spot.

People dig. Water comes up. Everybody thinks a miracle has been performed. But has it? Actually the people have been taken in by this so-called miracle. The water didn't come up because the diviner had a mysterious power. It came up because there is water under the ground almost everywhere—if you dig and drill deep enough. Some distance beneath the surface, the ground is saturated with water. There are even streams under the ground.

All this hidden water is very hard working. And in one way it actually accomplishes more than surface water does; for underground water dissolves much vaster quantities of minerals out of the rocks. It can do that because it takes its time—instead of just flowing over the rocks, it percolates slowly through them.

Like surface water, underground water carries the dissolved minerals toward the sea. And there a most amazing thing happens. In the sea the dissolved minerals are turned into rock! This rock is sedimentary rock—but it is not like conglomerate, sandstone and shale. It is not made out of pieces worn away from older rocks. It is made of materials that were once dissolved.

"But how can that be?" you may ask. "If minerals are dissolved, how can they become solid again?"

If something happens to the water, they can become solid again. That is something you can prove to yourself by making a simple experiment.

Put salt in a glass of water and stir it. You will find that all the salt will dissolve—provided you haven't put in too much. The water will stay clear, it will remain the same color, but it will taste salty. So although you can't see it, you can be sure the salt is still there.

Now, what do you do to get it back into a solid?

You let the water evaporate.

When the water goes away, a ring of salt will appear on the glass.

SELECTION 24

Purpose: To recall specific details in logical sequence.
Procedure: Read the selection and note the most important details as rapidly as possible. After reading the selection, refer to your notes and write in outline form, in the space provided, the most important details. Use complete sentences.

(385 words)

Finding Water

YOU MAY have heard that certain people have the mysterious power of finding water underground. They do it by means of a forked stick which they call a divining rod. The water diviner holds the two ends of the stick in his hands and walks along. Sud-

Anne Terry White. *All About Our Changing Rocks.* Copyright 1955 by Anne Terry White. Reprinted by permission of Random House, Inc. Pp. 87–9.

In the space below, list the important details you noted.

_____

_____

_____

_____

_____

_____

_____

_____

_____

_____

_____

_____

_____

_____

SELECTION 25

Purpose: To recall main ideas and the related important details in logical sequence.
Procedure: Read rapidly to locate the main idea in the following selection and then underline it. At the same time notice the important details related to the main idea. After reading the selection, refer to your underlinings made while reading and write down in outline form the main idea and related specific details.

(178 words)

Secrecy

THE MOST imposing argument against secrecy in a legislative body is that there is no such thing. Members do not have a choice between the fullest secrecy and the fullest publicity. They have a choice between complete, accurate, and honest reports of a proceeding and distorted, inaccurate hearsay reports of a proceeding. The committees can close the doors, but they seldom can close, utterly, the mouths of their members. They have a choice between an open meeting, fully and accurately reported to all the people; or a closed meeting, reported with varying degrees of accuracy to different groups of the people. So far as such reports are incorrect, they mislead and confuse citizens as to the merits of legislation and the virtues of lawmakers. So far as they are accurate for some citizens and inaccurate for others, these reports constitute a kind of discrimination, and a sort of favoritism that ought to be odious in a democracy.

In the space below write down the main idea of this selection. Then in outline form beneath the main idea, write the important details related to it.

_____

_____

_____

_____

_____

_____

_____

_____

_____

_____

_____

_____

_____

_____

_____

VOCABULARY EXERCISE V—*Selections 21–25*

Prefixes
Underline the prefix in each of the following words. Define each prefix and write other words containing the same prefix.

Word	Meaning	Other words
universe		
undertaken		
interlaces		
performed		
mislead		

Suffixes
Underline the suffix in each of the following words. Define each suffix and write other words containing the same suffix.

Word	Meaning	Other words
thoughtful		
physiology		
prettier		
sedimentary		
legislative		

Roots
Underline the root of each of the following words. Write the source word from which the root was derived and its meaning. Then write other words that have the same root.

Word	Source word	Meaning	Other words
gravity			
centuries			
anatomy			
divining			
conglomerate			

Synonyms
For each of the words listed below find other words that have the same or nearly the same meaning. If you wish to see the word used in context, make use of the selection and paragraph numbers indicated.

Word	Selection	Paragraph	Synonyms
principle	21	2	
professors	22	4	
nibbled	23	1	
percolates	24	3	
constitute	25	1	

Antonyms

For each of the words listed below find other words that have the opposite meaning. If you wish to see the word used in context, make use of the selection and paragraph numbers indicated.

Word	Selection	Paragraph	Antonyms
major	21	1	_____
popular	22	1	_____
shabby	23	1	_____
surface	24	3	_____
hearsay	25	1	_____

For your information

By adding affixes, i.e. prefixes or suffixes, to stems, we have greatly increased the number of useful words in our language. A good example: by adding the prefixes *re, con,* and *pre* to the stem *ced* we form the words recede, concede, and precede. What prefixes or suffixes can be added to the following stems to form various words?

1. vis   _____
2. aud   _____
3. duc   _____
4. dic   _____
5. ced   _____

6. fin   _____
7. ann   _____
8. port   _____
9. cap   _____
10. scrib   _____

SELECTION 26

Purpose: To recall main ideas and the related important details in logical sequence.
Procedure: Read rapidly to locate, and then underline the main idea in the following selection. At the same time notice the important details related to the main idea. After reading the selection in this manner, and without again referring to it, write in outline form the main idea and related specific details.

(183 words)

The Turning Point

EIGHTEEN HUNDRED and fifteen is a turning-point in American as in European history; and a point of divergence between them. Up to that time the development of the United States had been vitally affected by European forces. In spite of independence, colonial rivalries and maritime com-

Samuel Eliot Morison and Henry Steele Commager. *The Growth of the American Republic,* 4th ed. Copyright 1950 by Oxford University Press, Inc. P. 432.

merce kept the contact warm between the two worlds, and the European war had been projected into America. With the Peace of Vienna, Europe turned to problems that had little interest for America; and with the Peace of Ghent, America turned her back on the Atlantic. Every serious difficulty under which the young republic had labored since the War of Independence dropped out of sight. With national union achieved, a balance between liberty and order secured, a trifling national debt, and a virgin continent awaiting the plow, there opened a serene prospect of peace, prosperity, and social progress. No one suspected that expansion would bring its problems no less than encircling pressure, that the "self-evident truths" of the Declaration of Independence would be challenged anew, and that within half a century Americans would be slaughtering one another in the valleys of Virginia, and the rolling farmlands of Pennsylvania.

In the space below write down the main idea of this selection and the important details related to it.

_____

_____

_____

_____

_____

_____

_____

_____

_____

_____

_____

_____

_____

SELECTION 27

Purpose: To determine the author's point of view or purpose.
Procedure: Read to ascertain the author's point of view. Be ready to react to it.

(416 words)

The Grand Canyon

OUT IN our Southwest lies a great natural wonder—the Grand Canyon of the Colorado River. Every year thousands of tourists come from all over the world to see it. But though they "oh" and "ah" over the sight, not many really understand what it is they are looking at. The Grand Canyon

Anne Terry White. *All About Our Changing Rocks.* Copyright 1955 by Anne Terry White. Reprinted by permission of Random House, Inc. Pp. 32–4.

of the Colorado is the world's most gigantic example of rocks destroyed by water and wind and air.

You stand on the rim of the Grand Canyon and look out. Before you is a giant chasm that stretches as far as you can see. It is more than eight miles wide. It is three hundred miles long. And it is a mile deep. Down at the bottom flows the Colorado River which looks quite unimportant.

You look out and it seems to you that what you are seeing is not a chasm but two ranges of mountains. The top of each mountain is flat, and each is made of layer upon layer of rock. You can see the layers distinctly, for they are of different colors— some red, some green, some gray, some white. The whole scene looks as if it were cut out of gaily colored cardboard.

What does it all mean? What is the explanation of this wonder?

That unimportant looking river a mile below you is responsible for what has happened here. Once there was no chasm. The river flowed at the level where you stand. The Colorado is a very muddy river. It has used its silt and mud and stones as tools to saw and drill and grind its way down through a mile of rock. The streams that flow into the Colorado have cut the side canyons. With the help of air and rain and sun and frost and wind, the Colorado River and its tributaries have carved mountains out of the Colorado Plateau. It took a million years for them to do it.

How much rock did they destroy in that time?

You can get some notion of it from how much rock waste the Colorado carries away right now. Every hour it takes to the sea 11,000 tons of mud and stones! It has been doing that twenty-four hours a day, seven days a week for a million years!

But this is not the end yet. This is only a halfway point, for the Colorado and its tributaries are still sawing and drilling and grinding. Bit by bit the mountains will shrink still more. Bit by bit they will be carried out to sea.

In the space below, write out the author's point of view or belief.

———————————————————
———————————————————
———————————————————
———————————————————
———————————————————
———————————————————
———————————————————

SELECTION 28

Purpose: To determine the author's point of view or purpose.
Procedure: Read to ascertain the author's purpose.

(403 words)

The Parachute Fall

THE FLYER watches it out of the corner of his eye and fingers the D-ring that opens his parachute. "Hold it!" he warns himself. "Not up here. You are free-falling at around 300 miles per hour in this thin air. If you open your chute at that speed, the shock will either break you to pieces or rip the chute to shreds. Besides, it would take you some twenty minutes to get down to 10,000 feet. Oxygen supply in your bail-out bottle would never last while you floated down to breathable air. Not that it would make any difference; you'd be frozen stiff long before that time. Just keep your hand off that D-ring. This is no low-altitude jump."

The flyer has often wondered whether he would even be able to think, let alone think logically, during an emergency such as this. But he has listened to others tell about how clearly one's mind reacts at times like these. Now he knows they spoke the truth. The

From *Survival in the Sky* by Charles Coombs. © 1956 by Charles Coombs. By permission of William Morrow & Co., Inc. Pp. 30–32.

worst is over. All he needs to do now is let himself fall.

In the parachute pack on his back there is an aneroid device which is triggered by increased barometric pressure at low altitude. When he kicked away the seat, a lanyard attached to the parachute release prepared it to open automatically when the pilot would reach the safely thick atmosphere at 12,000 feet. By that time he would be out of the cold and out of danger from oxygen starvation. The denser air would also have lessened his falling speed to around 130 miles per hour, well within the safety limits for parachute opening.

So for nearly two minutes the pilot occupies himself with his thoughts, as he free-falls downward through 30,000 feet of rarefied air. It is bitterly cold. Although somewhat confined by the stiffness of his inflated pressure suit, he keeps exercising.

Just about the time the flyer is able to get a clear view of the fast-approaching ground, he feels a sudden lightness. With a loud pop that jerks him to a near-standstill, the main parachute blossoms out over his head.

Swinging securely beneath the comforting 28-foot canopy, the Super Sabre pilot now checks the terrain beneath him, guiding himself away from a clump of trees by gently tugging the shrouds, until at last he reaches earth.

In the space provided below, state the author's purpose in writing this selection.

———————————————————
———————————————————
———————————————————
———————————————————
———————————————————
———————————————————
———————————————————
———————————————————

SELECTION 29

Purpose: To determine the author's point of view or purpose in writing the selection.
Procedure: Read the selection to ascertain the author's purpose.

(404 words)

The Great Decision

ONE MORNING during Whitsuntide, when Albert Schweitzer had gone home to Gunsbach for the holidays, he woke up thinking again of how much he had to be thankful for. From his window he could hear the songs of the birds and the peaceful sounds of a village just awakening. It was good to be back home again with his gentle, understanding parents and his sisters and brother. It was also good to be able to go to the University. He loved the room he had there at the College of St. Thomas, looking out on the quiet, walled-in garden with its large shade trees. His studies were more like a game to him now, planning and preparing each one in the way he did. He thought of the pleasant evenings, too, with Ernest Munch, the organist, going over the scores of the Bach cantatas and talking together of the way they were meant to be performed.

Again the question came to him when such thoughts as these ran through his head. Had he a right to this happiness? He felt now the same as he had when he was a child and had learned that George Nitschelm could not have nourishing broth such as he had for his supper. It was like a small cloud hovering on the horizon. He might turn away and forget it for a time, but it was still there, just the same, slowly growing and slowly coming closer. At last he knew that he could ignore it no longer. As long as there were people in the world suffering from pain and want, it was not enough that he should accept his own happiness and perfect health without a thought

for others. He had a strength that gave him power to work and study day and night without ever knowing what it was to feel tired. Now he must give this strength to help others. He had been spared pain. Now he must try in some way to ease the pain of others. He must carry his own share of the misery of the world, instead of turning his back upon it and living for himself alone. The meaning of words in the Bible, hidden from him until then, became clear. "Whosoever would save his life shall lose it, and whosoever shall lose his life for My sake, shall save it."

On that June morning, when the sun came slanting through the windows of his room at the manse, Albert Schweitzer made a resolution that became the turning point of his life. He was twenty-one then. He would spend the next nine years, until he was thirty, doing the things he wanted to do, such as keeping on with his studies in science and music, and working as a pastor, as his father did. After that, he would give up these things and devote the rest of his life to serving mankind in some more direct way. Just what that way would be and how he would go about it, he was not sure. But now that he had made his decision, he had a feeling of inward peace.

In the space provided below, state the author's purpose in writing this selection.

_____

_____

_____

_____

_____

_____

_____

_____

_____

From the book *All Men Are Brothers* by Charlie May Simon. Copyright, ©, 1956 by E. P. Dutton & Co., Inc. Reprinted by permission of the publishers. Pp. 69–70.

III—Improving Comprehension

INTRODUCTION

WE HAVE defined reading as the interpretation of written materials. Two processes are involved in reading: visual perception of the printed symbols and the mental processes of thinking of the meaning associated with those symbols. It is the second of these processes, thinking, with which we are largely concerned when we deal with the matter of comprehension. Comprehension, then, may be considered as an understanding of the meanings to be gained from printed material.

Research shows that when the two factors are properly considered, reading rate and comprehension are only slightly related. It is important for the reader to adjust his rate to the speed that will enable him to best understand the material in the light of the particular purpose for which he is reading.

If, for example, the purpose for reading a particular selection is to obtain a general understanding of the material, the reading rate can be extremely rapid. A rapid skimming may prove adequate in such cases to obtain the level or degree of comprehension desired. On the other hand, if the purpose for reading is to master the material completely in order to pass an examination on

the subject, a slow study type of reading will be necessary to reach the degree of comprehension commensurate with the purpose set.

There are many specific skills necessary for good comprehension. Five of these skills that the authors think are the most crucial will be dealt with in the following pages. They are:

A. Locating key words.
B. Identifying main ideas.
C. Outlining, i.e. organizing the contents of written material in a logical sequence in respect to main ideas and supporting details.
D. Summarizing, i.e. the pulling together the main ideas of a selection into a concise, meaningful form.
E. Critical reading or analyzing of material to determine whether or not the reader and author are in agreement on the points of view presented, if the ideas presented are facts or opinions, and for what purpose the author is writing.

On the following pages are reading selections which will permit you to practice and develop competence in handling these five comprehension skills.

KEY WORDS

SELECTION 30

Purpose: To identify key words or phrases.
Procedure: Read the selection rapidly. As you do so, *underline* the key words or

phrases in each sentence. These are the words which give a specific meaning and tone to the material. If they were deleted or other words substituted for them the meaning would be changed greatly.

The Value of Education

(161 words)

THE EAGERNESS with which young men who had served in World War II accepted the educational opportunities offered by the GI Bill or Rights was not surprising. They had seen our country come out ahead in the great struggle, and they realized that back of this success was something more even than their own bravery and endurance on the field of battle. They had seen similar courage on the part of their enemies. They recognized the importance of the vast productive power of our country and the value of the new weapons being put in their hands. It was clear that it was the skill of millions of workers, the know-how of the engineers, and the administrative competence of our industrial and military leaders that transformed their willing courage into victory. They wanted to have their own part in these great developments. They saw in education the first essential step toward sharing more fully in the life of their country.

Arthur Holly Compton. *Atomic Quest.* Copyright 1956 by Oxford University Press, Inc. P. 337.

After reading Selection 30, note the words you have underlined. Do they include, among others, the following?

Sentence 1—eagerness, was not
         2—bravery
         4—importance
         5—victory
         6—wanted
         7—more

In order to appreciate the effect these words have upon the meaning and tone of the selection, substitute a word or phrase of opposite meaning. For example, for brave we could substitute cowardice, for victory, defeat.

Key words underlined   *Substitute*

——————————   ——————————

——————————   ——————————

Key words underlined   *Substitute*

——————————   ——————————

——————————   ——————————

——————————   ——————————

——————————   ——————————

——————————   ——————————

——————————   ——————————

——————————   ——————————

——————————   ——————————

——————————   ——————————

——————————   ——————————

——————————   ——————————

——————————   ——————————

——————————   ——————————

SELECTION 31

Purpose: To identify key words or phrases.
Procedure: Read the selection rapidly. As you do so, *underline* the key words or phrases in each sentence. After completing the selection note the words you have underlined. In order to appreciate the effect these words have upon the meaning and tone of the selection, list each one in the space provided and then substitute another word of opposite meaning for each.

(164 words)

The War Against Japan

As A matter of hard fact all competent reports about what was happening in Japan during the critical days of the summer of 1945 describe a situation in which the control of the Japanese government was hotly contested and surrender was extremely difficult to achieve. The defeat of Japan was

Arthur Holly Compton. *Atomic Quest.* Copyright 1956 by Oxford University Press, Inc. Pp. 261–2.

Key words underlined	Substitute

inevitable. This, however, had been true also for Iwo Jima and Okinawa, but control of these islands was not finally achieved without the almost complete destruction of the defending Japanese armies and with heavy cost to the American troops. A similar situation would almost certainly have developed in Japan proper. A month after the American occupation began, General MacArthur expressed the view that if the Japanese government should lose control its soldiers could begin a guerilla warfare requiring for its suppression ten years of fighting by a million American troops. Our costly experience had shown us what they meant when they said they would all have been killed but would not have been defeated.

VOCABULARY EXERCISE VI—*Selections 26–31*

Prefixes

Underline the prefix in each of the following words. Define each prefix and write other words containing the same prefix.

Word	Meaning	Other words
unimportant		
reacts		
education		
inevitable		

Suffixes

Underline the suffix in each of the following words. Define each suffix and write other words containing the same suffix.

Word	Meaning	Other words
explanation		
breathable		
lightness		
importance		

Roots

Underline the root of each of the following words. Write the source word from which the root was derived and its meaning. Then write other words that have the same root.

Word	Source word	Meaning	Other words
tributaries	_____	_____	_____
barometric	_____	_____	_____
endurance	_____	_____	_____
military	_____	_____	_____
occupation	_____	_____	_____

Synonyms

For each of the words listed below find other words that have the same or nearly the same meaning. If you wish to see the word used in context, make use of the selection and paragraph numbers indicated.

Word	Selection	Paragraph	Synonyms
chasm	27	2	_____
silt	27	5	_____
terrain	28	6	_____
essential	30	1	_____

Antonyms

For each of the words listed below find other words that have the opposite meaning. If you wish to see the word used in context, make use of the selection and paragraph numbers indicated.

Word	Selection	Paragraph	Antonyms
shrink	27	8	_____
denser	28	3	_____
vast	30	1	_____
bravery	30	1	_____

For your information

Our words have come from many languages besides Latin and Greek. For example, each of the following words comes directly or indirectly from another language.

Word	Language	Word	Language
nickel	German	piano	Italian
rodeo	Spanish	grotesque	French
yacht	Dutch	Sabbath	Hebrew
ski	Scandanavian		

As you study our language you will learn that words of a certain type come from certain sources. For example, the following words, all related to *music,* come from *Italian:* piano, solo, concerto, arta, stanza, oratorio. Select another language which has contributed to ours and see if the words it contributed relate to a certain topic, art, sport, or industry.

SELECTION 32

Purpose: To identify key words or phrases.
Procedure: Read the selection rapidly. As you do so, *underline* the key words or phrases in each sentence. After completing the selection note the words you have underlined. In order to appreciate the effect these words have upon the meaning and tone of the selection, list each one in the space provided and then substitute another word of opposite meaning for each.

(143 words)

The Ocean Floor

MANY PEOPLE think of the ocean as a huge basin filled with water. Since the water's surface is smooth and level, they assume that the ocean's bottom is smooth and level, too. Actually, this isn't so at all. The ocean's floor is full of underwater valleys, hills, and mountains. Sometimes the tops of these hills and mountains project up out of the water, forming islands. Others may not quite reach the surface; we know them as reefs.

A reef is a natural obstruction which lies at, or just beneath the surface of the water. This may be a sand ridge, or a chain of rocks. Some reefs are exposed by low tide, and covered by high tide, at which time it may be safe to pass over them. Others may be barely submerged by high water, in which case they are very dangerous.

Harry Zarchy. *Let's Go Boating.* Copyright 1952 by Alfred A. Knopf, Inc. P. 99.

Key words underlined   *Substitute*

_____   _____

_____   _____

_____   _____

_____   _____

_____   _____

_____   _____

SELECTION 33

Purpose: To identify key words or phrases.
Procedure: Read the selection rapidly. As you do so, *underline* the key words or phrases in each sentence. After completing the selection note the words you have underlined. In order to appreciate the effect these words have upon the meaning and tone of the selection, list each one in the space provided and then substitute another word of opposite meaning for each.

(121 words)

Tides

EVERYONE WHO has been to the seashore knows that the ocean's level rises and falls; these are the tides. They are caused by a pulling force that is exerted upon the earth by the sun and the moon. As the moon revolves around the earth, the water on the earth's surface tends to shift in the same direction.

Twice every 24 hours and 51 minutes, the ocean level at any one place rises to high tide, and recedes to low tide. The movement of water from low to high level is known as flood tide. At this time, water flows in toward shore, filling the bays, and even running up into rivers. Ebb tide occurs as the water level drops from high to low, and the water flows away from the shore.

Harry Zarchy. *Let's Go Boating.* Copyright 1952 by Alfred A. Knopf, Inc. P. 98.

Key words underlined   *Substitute*

_____   _____

_____   _____

_____   _____

_____   _____

_____   _____

_____   _____

MAIN IDEAS

SELECTION 34

Purpose: Read to select the *main idea* of the paragraph.

Procedure: Read the following paragraph as rapidly as possible in order to identify the main idea. Then complete the exercise following the selection.

(124 words)

The Atomic Bomb

THE ATOMIC weapons were only one of many factors which brought about the fall of Japan. The Japanese Navy had been destroyed. The blockade was choking the nation's economy. The Russian attack in Manchuria seems to have added to the feeling that nothing was to be gained by prolon ig the war. It was the combined effect of all of these disasters and many more that persuaded the Japanese to accept surrender. As Churchill had emphasized, however, the atomic bombs were something so completely out of the field of ordinary reckoning that they had taken matters away from Japan's control. The unique and probably crucial value of the atomic attack was that it afforded the Japanese people an opportunity to resign from the war with honor.

Arthur Holly Compton. *Atomic Quest.* Copyright 1956 by Oxford University Press, Inc. P. 262.

The main idea of this passage is best set forth in which one of the following statements?

___ 1. The atomic attack allowed the Japanese to surrender with honor.

___ 2. The atomic bomb was the one most important factor in the fall of Japan.

___ 3. According to Churchill, the government of Japan lost control after the atomic attack.

___ 4. A number of disasters forced Japan to surrender.

SELECTION 35

Purpose: Read to select the *main idea* of the paragraph.

Procedure: Read the following paragraph as rapidly as possible in order to identify the main idea. Then complete the exercise following the selection.

(122 words)

New Role for Colonial Power

AN ENCOURAGING aspect of the development of the new nationalism is the friendly relationship that has developed between certain of the so-called colonial nations and the powers that gave them their independence. The brightest example of this situation is perhaps the relation between the Philippines and the United States. The high respect also in which Britain is held by her former colonies of Pakistan and India is reflected by the way in which these are taking their part in the British Commonwealth of Nations. In these cases, the friendliness of the relationship is due largely to a recognition of the very substantial help that the former controlling powers have given to the new nations in preparing them for independent self-government.

Arthur Holly Compton. *Atomic Quest.* Copyright 1956 by Oxford University Press, Inc. Pp. 292–3.

The main idea of this passage is best set forth in which one of the following statements?

___ 1. The friendly relationship between the Philippines and the United States is a good example of what can happen between a colonial power and a former colony.

___ 2. Good relationships exist between new nations and the powers that gave them their independence when the great powers help prepare the new government for independence.

— 3. The British insured a good relationship between themselves and their former colonies by taking them into the British Commonwealth of Nations.

SELECTION 36

Purpose: Read to select the *main idea* of the paragraph.
Procedure: Read the following paragraph as rapidly as possible in order to identify the main idea. Then complete the exercise following the selection.

(54 words)

Genius of the Mormons

ALTHOUGH POLYGAMY was the feature of Mormonism that attracted popular attention, it was little more than a recruiting device appropriate for a wandering tribe and was finally abandoned in 1890. The genius of the Mormons lay in a disciplined community life, integrated by a peculiar faith and directed by able men of action.

Samuel Eliot Morison and Henry Steele Commager. *The Growth of the American Republic,* 4th ed. Copyright 1950 by Oxford University Press, Inc. P. 575.

The main idea of this passage is best set forth in which of the following statements?
— 1. Polygamy was a popular feature of Mormonism.
— 2. The Mormons were geniuses in recruiting new members.
— 3. The greatness of the Mormons lay in the fact that able men directed a disciplined community life integrated by their faith.

SELECTION 37

Purpose: Read to select the *main idea* of the paragraph.
Procedure: Read the following paragraph as rapidly as possible in order to identify the main idea. Then complete the exercise following the selection.

(104 words)

Rowboats

MOST PEOPLE think of rowboats as small craft, but this hasn't always been so. The ancient Egyptians and Phoenicians rowed their boats. The Greeks and Romans rigged sails on their mighty galleys, but the galleys were also propelled by oars. The famous Viking ships had sails, but there were many occasions when the mighty blond warriors used oars as their only means of propulsion. Until the art of using the sail to go against the wind was perfected, even large ships were equipped with oars. For many hundreds of years, men took to the oars in the absence of favorable winds.

Harry Zarchy. *Let's Go Boating.* Copyright 1952 by Alfred A. Knopf, Inc. P. 3.

In the space below write in your own words a sentence that expresses the main idea of the paragraph. (Compare your sentence with that found below.)

_____

_____

_____

(Rowing remained the principal power for driving boats for hundreds of years.)

OUTLINING

SELECTION 38

Purpose: To read the selection in order to develop a general outline of the material.

Procedure: Read the following selection as rapidly as you can. As you read, jot down the *main points* in the wide margin provided for this purpose. When you have completed the selection in this manner, use the space provided to write an outline of the main points. Leave space under each main point. After completing this portion of the outline go back and fill in as many details as you can *recall* that are related to each main point listed. Do not refer to the selection again until you have listed all the details you can recall. After listing all the details you can recall, you will want to look again at the selection to see if there are any details you omitted.

(406 words)

Salerno Medical School

FORTUNATELY THERE survived during the whole of this bleak period of the Middle Ages a small centre in Europe in which the lamps of Greek culture still continued to burn brightly and where medical progress was occasionally made. It was in the tiny town of Salerno, not very far from Naples. In Roman times Salerno had been a fashionable health resort and after the fall of the Roman Empire it had served as a convenient meeting-ground for people of culture. There are two legends concerning the origin of the medical school in Salerno; one, that it was founded by Charlemagne, and another, that it was started by "four masters," Elinus the Jew, Pontus the Greek, Adale the Arab, and Salernus the Latin. The latter legend, whether true or not, is at any rate in keeping with two of the chief characteristics of the Salernitan School: that it was open to men of all languages and of all nationalities and even to women; that it was a lay foundation and not a by-product of the neighbouring great monastery of Cassino. Not that there was any enmity between Salerno and the Church. On the contrary, there is every reason to believe that the physicians studying medicine at Salerno and the Benedictine Monks at Cassino were very friendly, and it is quite likely that the former were allowed to make use of the monastery's fine library.

The Medical School of Salerno came into being during the ninth century, was at its zenith at the beginning of the eleventh century and then slowly declined during the

Kenneth Walker. *The Story of Medicine.* Copyright 1954 by Kenneth Walker. Reprinted by permission of Oxford University Press. Pp. 75–6.

thirteenth century. It was famous throughout Europe and at one time to have studied at Salerno was sufficient to establish the medical reputation of any young physician. Salerno was also the first medical school to urge that people who practised medicine should hold some qualification for doing so. The decree setting this forth was issued in A. D. 1140 by Roger II of Sicily. "Whosoever will henceforth practise medicine, let him present himself to our officials and judges to be examined by them; but if he presume of his own temerity, let him be imprisoned and all his goods be sold by auction. The object of this is to prevent the subjects of our kingdom incurring peril through the ignorance of physicians."

The Medical School of Salerno gave useful instruction not only in medicine but in the ethics of medical practice.

Outline

(Use as many of the following spaces as needed.)

Main idea:
    Details:

_____

_____

_____

_____

Main idea:
    Details:

_____

_____

_____

_____

Main idea:
    Details:

_____

_____

_____

_____

Main idea:
   Details:

_____

_____

_____

_____

Main idea:
   Details:

_____

_____

_____

_____

VOCABULARY EXERCISE VII—*Selections 32–38*

Prefixes

Underline the prefix in each of the following words. Define each prefix and write other words containing the same prefix.

Word	*Meaning*	*Other words*
submerged		
prolonging		
imprisoned		
incurring		

Suffixes

Underline the suffix in each of the following words. Define each suffix and write other words containing the same suffix.

Word	*Meaning*	*Other words*
dangerous		
nationalism		
relationship		
throughout		

Roots

Underline the root of each of the following words. Write the source word from which the root was derived and its meaning. Then write other words that have the same root.

Word	Source word	Meaning	Other words
obstruction	_____	_____	_____
exerted	_____	_____	_____
economy	_____	_____	_____
atomic	_____	_____	_____
recognition	_____	_____	_____

Synonyms

For each of the words listed below find other words that have the same or nearly the same meaning. If you wish to see the word used in context, make use of the selection and paragraph numbers indicated.

Word	Selection	Paragraph	Synonyms
assume	32	1	_____
crucial	34	1	_____
galleys	37	1	_____
peril	38	2	_____

Antonyms

For each of the words listed below find other words that have the opposite meaning. If you wish to see the word used in context, make use of the selection and paragraph numbers indicated.

Word	Selection	Paragraph	Antonyms
recedes	33	2	_____
independent	35	1	_____
bleak	38	1	_____
progress	38	1	_____

For your information

There are a number of books that will prove of great help to you in improving your vocabulary.

Webster's New International Dictionary, an unabridged dictionary, is an important source of word meanings, pronunciation, and synonyms.

Webster's Dictionary of Synonyms is a presentation of synonyms of thousands of words in our language. In addition, analogous and contrasted words and antonyms are often presented. A typical example is the presentation of *accede.* Accede. Acquiese, assent, consent, agree, subscribe. Ana. Concur, co-operate (see UNITE): yield, submit, defer, relent: allow, permit, let. Ant. Demur—Con. Decline, refuse, reject, spurn: shy, stickle, strain, balk (see DEMUR): object, protest, kick: oppose, resist, withstand.

Roget's Thesaurus of English Words and Phrases is a book of synonyms and antonyms; invaluable as a source of words for the writer.

SELECTION 39

Purpose: To read the selection in order to develop a general outline of the material.
Procedure: Read the following selection as rapidly as you can. When you have finished reading, use the space provided to write an outline of the main points and the important details related to each main point. Do not refer to the selection again until after your outline has been completed.

(392 words)

The Place of Man in Aviation

THE HUMAN problems involved in adding each few miles of speed or each hundred feet of altitude to the flyer's realm of activity increase in almost direct proportion to increased performance. For this reason, aviation medicine—a new application of medical science—has become vitally important during the past ten or more years.

By combining its talents with science, research, and engineering, aviation medicine has taken an increasingly essential part in the dramatic and sometimes fantastic project of enabling man to remain master of his aircraft. Considering the spectacular advancements in modern aircraft, this is no easy assignment.

Why has man—almost overnight—become the big "if" in aviation? Why is so much concern suddenly centered upon him, instead of upon the airplane? Looking back, it is quite apparent that during the first fifty

From *Survival in the Sky* by Charles Coombs. © 1956 by Charles Coombs. By permission of William Morrow & Co., Inc. Pp. 33–6.

years of flight aviation was primarily a matter of building airplanes. There have been plenty of men eager and qualified to fly them ever since that December day in 1903 when Wilbur and Orville Wright managed to fly the first power-driven heavier-than-air craft off the sand dunes at Kitty Hawk, North Carolina. From that day onward, all efforts were directed toward building faster and higher-flying airplanes. There was no worry about the man inside the plane. If he had good vision, better than average co-ordination, a certain amount of training, and a flare for adventure, he could fill the pilot's seat. During most of those fifty years, airplanes flew at moderate speeds and altitudes, putting no exaggerated stresses or strains upon the pilot's mind or body. Consequently, nothing flyable had ever surpassed his ability to get it into the air and keep it there for a reasonable length of time.

But how true is that today? How true will it be tomorrow? So far, man has been able to keep up with the machine; he has remained master of the situation. But talk to any pilot of modern jet aircraft, and he is apt to smile wryly and admit that he sometimes wonders whether it is a matter of who is flying what or of what is flying whom.

During recent years the machine has had a definite tendency to take over the man. As yet it hasn't quite succeeded. But the threat is there—very positively there. And if the threat is there today, only fifty-plus years after the beginning of aviation, what about tomorrow? What is man's place in the future of aviation? At present, this is the area of greatest concern in the field of flight.

Outline

(Use as many of the following spaces as needed.)

Main idea:
    Details:

_____

_____

_____

_____

_____

Main idea:
  Details:

_____

_____

_____

_____

_____

Main idea:
  Details:

_____

_____

_____

_____

_____

Main idea:
  Details:

_____

_____

_____

_____

_____

Main idea:
  Details:

_____

_____

_____

_____

_____

SELECTION 40

Purpose: To read and reduce the material to convenient outline form.

Procedure: Read the selection carefully, keeping the above-mentioned purpose in mind. After reading the selection use the space provided to make an outline of the material similar to the one you made for Selection 39.

(524 words)

Radioactive Absorption

IT WAS not only with the health of people, however, that we were concerned. One morning as the Metallurgical Project Council was in session, Crawford Greenewalt, just arrived from Wilmington, asked for the floor. He opened his comments with one word: "Fish!" What would the cooling water, returning from the nuclear reactors into the Columbia River, do to the fish that were so important in the economy of the Northwest? This was a problem prominent in the mind of General Robbins, Deputy Chief of Engineers, who had spent considerable time as Division Engineer in the Columbia area.

Immediately experiments were undertaken. It was found that fish are unusually resistant to the direct effects of radiation. On the other hand, even with minute amounts of radioactive fission products present in the water surprisingly large amounts were absorbed and concentrated in their bones. In fact, a fish could thus be made so radioactive that its skeleton would mark itself on a photographic plate. It was clear that extreme precaution would be necessary in order to prevent any radioactive materials from reaching the Columbia River water. This became eventually a problem even with the lower level of operation at Oak Ridge. Special precautions were

Arthur Holly Compton. *Atomic Quest.* Copyright 1956 by Oxford University Press, Inc. Pp. 179–80.

necessary lest wastes from the chemical operations should impart radioactivity to the Clinch River.

A by-product of such studies was the discovery of the hazardous character of the chemical element plutonium itself. Radium poisoning had become a matter of public attention twenty years earlier as a result of its effects on a group of radium-dial painters. Its effects are caused by concentration of radium in the bone. There it destroys the structures that produce the red blood corpuscles and produces an anemia which, if sufficiently severe, results in death. The fission products that arise from the fission of uranium are mostly so short-lived that they do not produce any persistent effects of this kind. Radium, however, has a half life of about two thousand years and thus does not decay appreciably during a person's lifetime. The only effective treatment for radium poisoning is to displace the radium from the bone and then attempt to replace it by calcium, a slow, tedious, difficult process.

Experiments with animals showed that plutonium also deposits itself in the bone. Like radium, it emits alpha particles which are capable of destroying the source of red blood cells, and plutonium retains its radioactivity ten times longer than does radium. What is more, plutonium emits only very feeble gamma rays. It is the gamma rays emitted by radium that tell us how much of this substance is in a person's body. Because this method is not useful for detecting the presence of plutonium, its effects are very insidious. Other means of detection have been developed, but these are not always reliable. The net result is that those who work with plutonium need to take extreme precautions. It is precisely such precautions that have occupied much of the attention of those concerned with protection against radiation hazards. Thus, for more reasons than one, plutonium is one of the most dangerous, as well as one of the most valuable, of the substances known to man.

Outline

In the space below develop an outline of the contents of the selection you have just read.

_____

_____

_____

_____

_____

_____

_____

_____

_____

_____

_____

_____

_____

_____

_____

_____

_____

_____

_____

_____

_____

_____

_____

_____

_____

_____

_____

_____

_____

_____

_____

_____

_____

_____

_____

SELECTION 41

Purpose: To read and reduce the material to convenient outline form.

Procedure: Read the selection carefully, keeping the above purpose in mind. After reading the selection use the space provided to make an outline of the material similar to the ones you made for Selections 39 and 40.

(386 words)

The Louisiana Purchase

THE LOUISIANA Purchase has been called "the greatest real estate bargain in history." That estimate is probably correct. At any rate, it would be hard to think of a better one, though the United States has always done pretty well in its real estate deals. Manhattan Island wasn't a bad buy. Neither was Alaska nor the Gadsden Purchase.

But the Louisiana Purchase was a good deal more than a smart bargain in real estate. It was really the making of the modern United States; or, if that is putting it too strongly, it was one of half a dozen events, without which there would never have been anything like the present United States of America.

The Louisiana Purchase made possible the destiny of America as a two-ocean world power. It gave us control of some of the most fertile territory and some of the

Earl Schenck Miers. *The American Story.* Copyright 1956 by Channel Press, Inc. Pp. 108–9.

richest mines in the world. It gave us control of the Mississippi River, which, in the days before transportation by air and rail, was a vital commercial route. Thus the Louisiana Purchase united our country as nothing else could have done. The West— in those days that meant Kentucky and the country around it—decided to stick with the United States. Before the Purchase there had been continual trouble because farm products could be sold only by sending them down the Mississippi, with the Spaniards in control of New Orleans. Western Pennsylvania even staged an armed rebellion, which had to be suppressed by the father of Robert E. Lee! There was always the chance that the Westerners might leave the United States entirely and throw in their lot with Spain. Even so sterling an American as Daniel Boone had been forced to leave the country he had opened up, and settle in Missouri, then part of "Louisiana." Boone was even, for a time, an official of the Spanish government in Missouri.

But when the Louisiana Purchase made the Mississippi firmly American, as well as the vast stretch of country reaching to the Rockies, the United States could turn its back on the Atlantic world and forget the squabbles of Europe for at least a century. We could devote ourselves to developing our own immense resources and immense internal market, unhampered by tariffs between the states, or frontier jealousies. We could provide for a growing population.

Outline

In the space below develop an outline of the contents of the selection you have just read.

_____

_____

_____

_____

_____

_____

_____

_____

_____

_____

_____

_____

_____

_____

_____

_____

_____

_____

_____

_____

_____

_____

_____

_____

_____

SUMMARIZING

IN THE preceding exercises you have been given practice in determining main ideas and their supporting details. In the following selections you will be asked not only to perform these same tasks but also to make use of the main ideas and supporting details in reducing the material to a handy summary form.

SELECTION 42

Purpose: To read and reduce the material to a handy summary form.

Procedure: Read the following paragraph as quickly as you can. When you are finished check the statement that best expresses the main idea of the selection. Then, in the space provided, jot down the key phrases that serve as supporting details to the main

idea. Finally, using the main idea and the supporting details you have listed, write a summary of the selection. Limit your summary to a maximum of 50 words.

(147 words)

Trade Barriers and Japanese Prosperity

JAPAN IS a nation that is particularly hard-hit by trade barriers. Shortage of land area and raw materials makes it impossible for her to provide her necessities from within. International trade she must have. But in all too many parts of the world her products run into quotas, complex and changing

Arthur Holly Compton. *Atomic Quest.* Copyright 1956 by Oxford University Press, Inc. Pp. 293–4.

customs regulations, and high import duties. Japan, has, however, much to offer the world. The health and prosperity of the nations, including especially our own, call for sympathetic attention to her difficult situation. The Japanese in their entire approach to life are as far from the ideas of Communism as it is possible for a people to be. Yet if the door to the remainder of the free world is kept closed and that to the world of Communism is held open, Japan's economic survival will require that she make use of the door that is open.

Which one of the following statements best summarizes the preceding paragraph?
___ 1. Trade barriers to the free world will force Japan to trade with the Communist powers.
___ 2. The Japanese are as far from the ideas of Communism as a people can be.
___ 3. If Japan is to survive we must use an open door policy with her.
___ 4. Japan has a great deal to offer the world in manufactured goods and in trade for raw materials.

In the space below jot down the key phrases that serve as supporting details to the main idea.

_____

_____

_____

_____

_____

_____

Using the main idea and the supporting details you have listed, write a summary of the selection.

_____

_____

_____

_____

_____

_____

_____

_____

_____

_____

_____

_____

_____

SELECTION 43

Purpose: To read and reduce the material to a handy summary form.
Procedure: Read the following selection as quickly as you can. When you are finished check the statement that best expresses the main idea of the selection. Then, in the space provided, jot down the key phrases that serve as supporting details to the main idea. Finally, using the main idea and the supporting details you havel isted, write a summary of the selection. Limit your summary to a maximum of 50 words.

(210 words)

Good News

ONE EVENING after his return from a mysterious journey away from the hospital, Dr. Schweitzer called the two doctors and the two nurses together, saying that he had some news for them. He told how the hospital would be moved to a larger site, and explained that he had waited until he was sure of his plans before mentioning them. But now the District Commissioner had agreed to let the hospital have the use of the tract of land, a hundred and seventy-two acres, on the site of the old Galoa village.

At first his co-workers were speechless with surprise. Then they broke into shouts of joy, and all began talking at once. They made their plans then and there. There

From the book *All Men Are Brothers* by Charlie May Simon. Copyright, ©, 1956 by E. P. Dutton & Co., Inc. Reprinted by permission of the publishers. P. 157.

would be stronger buildings, space for isolation wards, space to spread out and grow, space to plant food for the sick and for themselves. But what an undertaking it would be! The place had gone back to jungle completely in the years since it had been abandoned.

The Africans standing near stared in astonishment. Never had they seen such gesticulations, or heard such chatter from these Europeans. It was like one of their own palavers when the men met and talked under the roof of their palaver houses.

Which of the following statements is the best summary of the selection just read?
— 1. Dr. Schweitzer's co-workers were surprised and delighted to hear the news of the new site.
— 2. Dr. Schweitzer returned from a mysterious journey with good news.
— 3. The noisy reaction of the Europeans to Dr. Schweitzer's announcement surprised the Africans.

In the space below jot down the key phrases that serve as supporting details to the main idea.

_____

_____

_____

_____

Using the main idea and the supporting details you have listed, write a summary of the selection.

_____

_____

_____

_____

_____

_____

_____

SELECTION 44

Purpose: To read and reduce the material to a handy summary form.

Procedure: With the above-mentioned purpose in mind, carefully read the following selection. In the space provided write down the main idea of the selection. Under the main idea jot down the key phrases which serve as supporting details to the main idea. Then, using the main idea and the supporting details you have listed, write a summary of the selection. Limit your summary to a maximum of 50 words.

(240 words)

Trade Channels

FOR A decade the waters of New York State had offered a thought-provoking pattern to the nation-builders at the beginning of the 19th century. Their dreams of moving the riches of the West to ports on the shores of the Atlantic were troubled. There was the possibility that the prized cargoes might move from Lake Erie into Lake Ontario and thence down the St. Lawrence River to British-Canadian markets. There was a stronger chance that the Mississippi might prove the major channel for transporting the treasures of the midlands to New Orleans. If the vast grain and beef producing plains and the ore-laden mountains were to be profitable to the East, home of the majority of the people, it would be necessary to conceive and execute a plan by which Lake Erie could be connected with

Earl Schenck Miers. *The American Story.* Copyright 1956 by Channel Press, Inc. P. 127.

other navigable waters that led to Atlantic ports. That this link must be forged as soon as possible was made very clear by President George Washington as early as 1784: "The Western settlers," he said, "stand as it were upon a pivot. The touch of a feather would turn them any way . . . smooth the road and make the way easy for them, and then see what an influx of articles will be poured upon us; how amazingly our exports will be increased by them, and how amply we shall be compensated for any trouble and expense we may encounter to effect it."

In the spaces provided below, write the main idea of the selection, the details supporting the main idea, and a summary of the selection.

Main idea:

_____

_____

_____

_____

_____

Supporting details:

_____

_____

_____

_____

_____

_____

_____

Summary:

_____

_____

_____

_____

_____

_____

_____

_____

_____

_____

_____

_____

SELECTION 45

Purpose: To read and reduce the material to a handy summary form.

Procedure: With the above-mentioned purpose in mind, carefully read the following selection. In the space provided write down the main idea of the selection. Under the main idea jot down the key phrases which serve as supporting details to the main idea. Then, using the main idea and the supporting details you have listed, write a summary of the selection. Limit your summary to a maximum of 50 words.

(600 words)

Conflict for an Idea

AT A distance of sixty years men wonder at the rash and hopeless gallantry of the Southern war for independence. A loose agrarian confederacy of five or six million whites and three and a half million slaves challenged a federal union of nineteen or twenty million freemen with overwhelming financial and industrial advantages. Yet, futile as the effort proved and tragic as the consequences, the Southern cause was not predestined to defeat.

The Confederacy, in order to win, needed merely to defend her own territory long enough to weary the Northerners of war.

Samuel Eliot Morison and Henry Steele Commager. *The Growth of the American Republic,* 4th ed. Copyright 1950 by Oxford University Press, Inc. Pp. 653–5.

The United States, in order to win, had to conquer an empire and crush a people. A negotiated peace, or any less emphatic result than unconditional surrender of the Southern armies and total collapse of the Confederate government, would have meant some sort of special privilege to the Southern states within the Union, if not independence without the Union: in either event a Southern victory. Material advantages were not all in favor of the Union. To offset the Northern superiority in numbers, wealth, industry, transportation, and sea-power, the Confederacy had the advantage of interior lines, a coast-line so long it almost defied blockade, a military tradition, and confident expectation of foreign assistance.

For the moral scales seemed to be weighted in favor of the South. From their point of view, Southerners were fighting for everything that men hold dear: liberty and self-government, hearth and home, the supremacy of their race. They could abandon the struggle only by sacrificing the very bases of their society; and defeat for them involved the most bitter humiliation to which any English-speaking people has been subjected. The Northern people, on the contrary, could have stopped the war at any moment, at the mere cost of recognizing what to many seemed an accomplished fact, and without any sacrifice of the solid and material factors that most closely touch the life of the individual. They were fighting merely for an idea and a sentiment, the sentiment of Union, which, translated into action, seemed to tender souls scarcely different from conquest. Negro emancipation, itself an ideal, came more as an incident than as an object of the war. It was not the abolitionist "Battle-Hymn of the Republic" that sent the blood leaping through Northern veins in those years of trial, but the simple sentiment of:

The Union forever, hurrah! boys, hurrah!
  Down with the traitor, up with the star,
While we rally round the flag, boys, rally once
    again,
  Shouting the battle-cry of Freedom.

Under these circumstances there was every reason to expect that the South would win. Europe as a whole so believed, as soon as the news of Bull Run seemed to prove that the South was in earnest, and that the North was not. The Thirteen Colonies, The Netherlands, and in recent memory the South American and the Italian states had achieved their independence against greater odds; and if Hungary had failed, it was because Russia threw her weight on the other side. Even devoted partisans of the American Union like John Bright hardly dared hope for its complete restoration; and among the statesmen, the military experts, the journalists, the men of letters, and leaders of public opinion in Western Europe, those who before the end of 1863 doubted the permanency of separation were few and inconspicuous. For there was one imponderable and unique factor of which almost everyone in Europe was ignorant: the steadfast devotion to the Union which alone made it possible for the superior material resources of the United States to prevail.

In the spaces provided below, write the main idea of the selection, the details supporting the main idea, and a summary of the selection.

Main idea:

_____

_____

_____

_____

_____

Supporting details:

_____

_____

_____

_____

_____

_____   _____

_____   _____

_____   _____

_____   _____

Summary: _____

_____   _____

_____   _____

_____   _____

CRITICAL READING

SELECTION 46

Purpose: To determine the author's point of view.

Procedure: Read to ascertain the author's point of view. Be ready to react to it.

(214 words)

The Garden of Eden

As THE work went on, the doctor could see the dream take shape that he had cherished for a long time. Some day the place would be a Garden of Eden with hundreds of fruit trees started from seeds. He would have every kind of fruit and vegetable that could be grown in a tropical climate. Here in this land where nature had provided no edible plant, where everything that bore fruit or leaf or root for food had been brought here and transplanted, there would now be food for all. There would be oil to cook it in from the oil palms left standing. And a herd of goats would be brought in, bred to resist the tsetse fly, so there would be milk for the sick and the orphan babies. Perhaps there would even be a time when food would be so plentiful that everyone could take all he wanted, and there would be no more hunger and famine, and no crime of stealing to eat.

Slowly the hospital buildings themselves began to take shape. There was much that

From the book *All Men Are Brothers* by Charlie May Simon. Copyright, ©, 1956 by E. P. Dutton & Co., Inc. Reprinted by permission of the publishers. Pp. 159–60.

the doctor had learned in the years since he had first come to the tropics, and it was well he had this experience behind him before starting to build a permanent hospital.

You have read *The Garden of Eden*. Write a brief statement that summarizes the doctor's belief.

_____

_____

_____

_____

_____

_____

Do you believe this to be a practical belief? Give reasons for believing as you do.

_____

_____

_____

_____

_____

_____

_____

_____

is a very solid molecular structure compared to the real nothingness of space. Not only does it contain nature's only suitable source of life-sustaining oxygen; it is also solid and heavy enough to exert the barometric pressure necessary to hold the human body together. Man has lived in and become accustomed to atmospheric pressure since time began.

After reading *Man's Limitations* would you say that the author is optimistic or pessimistic about man's future progress in aviation? Do you agree with the author? If you think the author pessimistic about man's limitations, tell why you think so.

_____

_____

_____

_____

_____

_____

_____

_____

_____

_____

_____

_____

_____

_____

_____

_____

SELECTION 47

Purpose: To determine the author's point of view.
Procedure: Read to ascertain the author's point of view. Be ready to react to it.

(234 words)

Man's Limitations

PROGRESS IN aviation, however, has been measured almost entirely by improvements in the machine, not in the man. Man's physical limitations are fairly constant factors, although not always easy to measure, and flying applies various severe stresses and strains on the human body. Being pliable—often to an amazing degree—man can oppose those stresses and strains, but he can never fully overcome them. There will always be a point beyond which his most valiant efforts will fail to overcome the ever-increasing physical and mental loads imposed upon him by supersonic flight. Fortunately, this point of failure has never been definitely established. Some say it is in sight; others say not yet. But all aviation experts admit that man is finding it more and more difficult to adapt himself to the rigorous demands of faster and higher flight. Let's look at man for a moment and see why he is the weak link in this flying business. Man is designed to live comfortably only in the relatively dense atmosphere near the earth. As we all know, air

From *Survival in the Sky* by Charles Coombs. © 1956 by Charles Coombs. By permission of William Morrow & Co., Inc. Pp. 45–6.

SELECTION 48

Purpose: To determine the author's point of view.
Procedure: Read to ascertain the author's point of view. Be ready to react to it.

(228 words)

The Age of Great Moguls

WHAT IS the legacy of the Age of Enterprise? In its early years, public opinion regarded its leaders as builders. The spirit of

Earl Schenck Miers. *The American Story.* Copyright 1956 by Channel Press, Inc. Pp. 243–4.

the time was with them. Few doubted that Singer had been a benefactor in filling the world with sewing machines, McCormick in making reapers abundant, Carnegie in bringing the Bessemer process to America, Rockefeller in standardizing kerosene and giving American oil a world market against Russian competition, Westinghouse in popularizing electrical equipment.

In the muckraking years opinion changed; the Age of Enterprise came under the fiercest criticism. Now that big business is fairly tamed and most heads show a proper social sense, the pendulum has swung back again. On a few men, like Jay Gould, a lasting stigma has been placed. But we can see that a majority of the Great Enterprisers were builders. They gave the country an industrial plant which became indispensable to our high standard of living, and to our victory in two World Wars. Their Age of Enterprise raised our economy to the point where we produce 60 per cent of the wealth of the world. They enabled America to become the bulwark of the free world. That Age—the Age of the Great Moguls—belongs to history. For all its mistakes and sins, it accomplished its mission. How else could this have been done more quickly and efficiently? How else could it have been done with less human strain and suffering? It will be a bold man who essays an answer.

State in a few words the author's opinion of the Age of Great Moguls.

_____

_____

_____

_____

_____

_____

Do you agree with the author? Yes ___
No ___

If you do not agree, what is your point of view on the subject?

_____

_____

_____

_____

_____

_____

_____

_____

_____

_____

_____

SELECTION 49

Purpose: To determine the author's point of view.
Procedure: Read to ascertain the author's point of view. Be ready to react to it.

(99 words)

Ordinary Men

THE POWERS of ordinary men are circumscribed by the everyday worlds in which they live, yet even in these rounds of job, family, and neighborhood they often seem driven by forces they can neither understand nor govern. "Great changes" are beyond their control, but affect their conduct and outlook none the less. The very framework of modern society confines them to projects not their own, but from every side, such changes now press upon the men and women of the mass society, who accordingly feel that they are without purpose in an epoch in which they are without power.

C. Wright Mills. *The Power Elite.* Copyright 1956 by Oxford University Press, Inc. P. 3.

What is the author's point of view regarding "ordinary men"?

_____
_____
_____
_____
_____
_____
_____

Do you agree with the author? If you do not agree, describe your own feelings on the matter. Support your point of view with examples if possible.

_____
_____
_____
_____
_____
_____
_____

VOCABULARY EXERCISE VIII—*Selections 39–49*

Prefixes

Underline the prefix in each of the following words. Define each prefix and write other words containing the same prefix.

Word	Meaning	Other words
consequently	_____	_____
transplanted	_____	_____

Suffixes

Underline the suffix in each of the following words. Define each suffix and write other words containing the same suffix.

Word	Meaning	Other words
assignment	_____	_____
speechless	_____	_____
plentiful	_____	_____

Roots

Underline the root of each of the following words. Write the source word from which the root was derived and its meaning. Then write other words that have the same root.

Word	Source word	Meaning	Other words
altitude	_____	_____	_____
necessities	_____	_____	_____
communism	_____	_____	_____
agrarian	_____	_____	_____
influx	_____	_____	_____

Synonyms

For each of the words listed below find other words that have the same or nearly the same meaning. If you wish to see the word used in context, make use of the selection and paragraph numbers indicated.

Word	Selection	Paragraph	Synonyms
realm	39	1	_____
wryly	39	4	_____
abandoned	43	2	_____
partisans	45	4	_____

Antonyms

For each of the words listed below find other words that have the opposite meaning. If you wish to see the word used in context, make use of the selection and paragraph numbers indicated.

Word	Selection	Paragraph	Antonyms
definite	39	5	_____
agreed	43	1	_____
futile	45	1	_____
navigable	44	1	_____

For your information

There are many books that will help you extend your knowledge of our language. We should like to recommend two:

Mathews, M. M. *Words, How to Know Them,* Henry Holt & Company, New York, 1956.
Radke, Frieda. *Word Resources.* The Odyssey Press, Inc., New York, 1955.

After you have read these two books, your appetite will be whetted for further study of our complex language.

IV—Applying Efficient Reading in College

A WEEK OF READING AT COLLEGE

THE AVERAGE college student takes from five to seven different subjects each semester. Some subjects, such as literature, citizenship education, and zoology, require a considerable amount of reading. It is probable that a minimum of 20 hours of reading per week is required by the average student in order to maintain adequate grades.

Look at a class schedule of Joe, a college student.

(Sample Schedule)

Time	Monday	Tuesday	Wednesday	Thursday	Friday	Saturday
8:00	Zoology		Zoology		Zoology	
9:00		Physical Education		Physical Education		
10:00		Chemistry Lecture		Chemistry Lecture		
11:00	Citizenship	Math. (Algebra)	Citizenship	Math. (Algebra)	Citizenship	
12:00						
1:00	English	Chemistry	English	Chemistry	English	
2:00	Zoology	Laboratory 1:15–4:00		Laboratory 1:15–4:00		
3:00	Laboratory 2:15–5:15					

In order to do the minimum amount of satisfactory work Joe must spend at least two hours per night reading. This total is based on the fact that Joe attends 14 hours of lecture each week and it is suggested that he study at least one hour for each lecture.

Joe is taking chemistry. His actual reading assignment for one week will probably cover one chapter in his text. It is probable that Joe will not find it too difficult to read the chemistry text because he is interested in the subject and is familiar with it because he has had a basic chemistry course in high school. As he advances in the course, however, Joe will find many unfamiliar terms. He will also study new facts, and be confronted with advanced ideas and concepts.

Zoology is a new subject for Joe. He has had no previous courses in the subject and knows very little about it. In addition to an extremely limited familiarity with the subject, Joe finds his interest in the zoology is far less than in his other courses.

Under these conditions Joe will probably find zoology a much more difficult course than chemistry. Nevertheless, he will have weekly readings that will cover as many, if not more, pages as the assignments in chemistry.

Joe is going to find that his familiarity and interest in other subjects will vary. In each subject he will find new facts and ideas as well as new vocabulary. His assignments will include many pages of textbook and additional recommended reading.

Joe's academic success in these courses is going to depend in part upon how efficiently and effectively he is able to read the assignments required by each of his professors.

In addition to employing the suggestions given in previous sections of this manual for reading short selections, it is now necessary for Joe to consider reading entire chapters and even complete texts. The following five-step approach is recommended for the reading of textbook assignments.

1. *Skim* the entire chapter or reading assignment in order to determine the main idea and other ideas covered. You will check such things as:

— chapter heading.

— introductory paragraph.

— key bits of information found in boldface type, also italicized words, dates, names.

— diagrams and illustrations.

— summarizing statements.

— end of the chapter questions.

This skimming requires only a few minutes but is an extremely valuable phase of an efficient reading pattern. It permits you to do the following important things before you begin to study:

— obtain a general over-all picture of what is covered in the reading assignment. This knowledge permits you to place in their proper perspective in relation to the entire chapter the various parts and ideas that will be encountered as you study the chapter.

— evaluate the material in respect to your familiarity with it.

— determine the difficulty level of the material.

— determine the author's purpose and viewpoint as expressed in the introductory and summary statements.

— determine those points the author feels are of sufficient importance to include in end of chapter questions.

2. Establish specific *purposes* for your reading by raising questions related to the section or paragraph headings. This can be most easily accomplished by merely turning section or paragraph headings into questions.

3. *Read* to answer the questions you have raised to help guide your purpose for reading. Keep your reading rate flexible. Remember your purpose for reading, the degree of your familiarity with the material, and the difficulty level of the material. Skim until you locate the answer to the question or questions you have established as the purpose for your reading. Then read slowly. Be sure you understand the answer. Read only to the end of the paragraph or section in which your question will be answered.

4. Look away from your book and see if, in your own words, you can *answer the questions* that have guided your reading. If you can answer the questions, move on to the next section. If you cannot answer the questions, or if you do not understand the answers, reread the section to locate and understand the answer.

During this fourth step you may wish to jot down notes for later reference.

After you have located the answers, understand them, and are able to restate them in your own words, go on to the next section and repeat steps number 2, 3, and 4. Continue through the entire reading assignment in this same manner.

5. Finally, *review* what you have read. After completing the reading assignment, put into practice the outlining and summarizing skills developed in Selections 38 through 45. If you are able to outline and summarize what you have read without referring back to the material, you can feel quite confident that you have mastered your reading assignment.

V—Post-Tests

FLEXIBILITY OF READING POST-TEST

NARRATIVE POST-TEST

Purpose: To read as quickly as you can and still understand the general content of this selection.

Procedure: Record the time (hour, minutes, seconds) when you begin reading the selection. After reading the selection, again record the time. Then answer the questions related to the selection.

Beginning Time:

Hour: _____ Minutes: _____ Seconds: _____

(810 words)

The Mary B.

THE MARY B. was like an oasis of life in miles of sea desert, a place where myriads of the sea's lesser fry—the small, backboneless animals—found a place of attachment; and the small fish foragers found living food encrusting all the planks and spars; and larger predators and prowlers of the sea found a hiding place.

The sea trout drew near to the dark hulk of the wreck as the last green light was fading to gray. They took some of the small fishes and crabs which they found about the vessel, satisfying the hunger born of the long, swift flight from the cold of the bay. Then they settled for the night near the weedy timbers of the Mary B.

The trout school lay in the water over the wreck in the lethargy that passed for sleep. They moved their fins gently to keep their position with relation to the wreck and to

Rachel L. Carson. *Under the Sea-Wind.* Copyright 1941 by Rachel L. Carson. Reprinted by permission of Oxford University Press. Pp. 240-44.

each other as the water pressed steadily over the shoal, moving up the slope from the sea.

At dusk the winding processions of small fishes that moved in and out of the deckhouse windows and through holes in the rotting planks dispersed and their members found resting places about the wreck. With the twilight which came early through the winter sea, the larger hunters who lived in and about the Mary B. stirred swiftly to life.

A long, snakelike arm was thrust out of the dark cavern of the fishhold, gripping the deck with double rows of suction cups. One after another, arms to the number of eight appeared, gripping the deck as a dark form clambered out of the hold. The creature was a large octopus who lived in the fishhold of the Mary B. It glided across the deck and slid into the recess above the lower wall of the deckhouse, where it concealed itself to begin the night's hunting. As it lay on the old, weed-grown planks its arms were never still, but reached out busily in all directions, exploring every familiar crack and crevice for unwary prey.

The octopus had not long to wait before a small cunner, intent on the mossy hydroids which it was nibbling off the planks of the vessel, came grazing along the wall of the deckhouse. The cunner, unsuspicious of danger, drew nearer. The octopus waited, its eyes fixed on the moving form, its groping arms stilled. The small fish came to the corner of the deckhouse, jutting out at a forty-five degree angle to the sea bottom. A long tentacle whipped around the corner and encircled the cunner with its sensitive tip. The cunner struggled with all its strength to escape the clasp of the suckers that adhered to scales, fins, and gill covers, but it was drawn down swiftly to the waiting

mouth and torn apart by the cruel beak, shaped like a parrot's.

Many times that night the waiting octopus seized unwary fish or crabs that strayed within reach of its tentacles, or launched itself out into the water to capture a fish passing at a greater distance. Then it moved by a pumping of its flaccid, saclike body, propelling itself by jets of liquid squirted from its siphons. Rarely did the encircling arms and gripping suction cups miss their mark, and gradually the gnawing hunger in the maw of the creature was assuaged.

When the weeds under the prow of the Mary B. were swaying confusedly to the turn of the tide, a large lobster emerged from its hiding place in the weed bed and moved off in a general shoreward direction. On land the lobster's unwieldy body would have weighed thirty pounds, but on the sea bottom it was supported by the water so that the creature moved nimbly on the tips of its four pairs of slender walking legs. The lobster carried the large crushing claws, or chelae, extended before its body, ready to seize its prey or attack an enemy.

Moving up along the vessel, the lobster paused to pick off a large starfish that was creeping over the mat of barnacles that covered the stern of the wreck with a white crust. The writhing starfish was conveyed by the pincer claws of the foremost walking legs to the mouth, where other appendages, composed of many joints and moving busily, held the spiny-skinned creature against the grinding jaws.

After eating part of the starfish, the lobster abandoned it to the scavenger crabs and moved on across the sand. Once it paused to dig for clams, turning over the sand busily. All the while its long, sensitive antennae were whipping the water for food scents. Finding no clams, the lobster moved into the shadows for its night's foraging.

Ending Time:

Hour: _____ Minutes: _____ Seconds: _____

NARRATIVE II—*The Mary B.*

Comprehension Check

Indicate whether, according to the selection just read, each of the following statements is true or false.

1. T F Sea trout fed on small fishes and crabs.
2. T F The octopus held its prey by means of suckers on the tip of its arms.
3. T F It was not possible for the giant octopus to satisfy its hunger.
4. T F The lobster moves in a nimble fashion on the bottom of the sea.
5. T F The octopus could only catch fish it could see.
6. T F The trout kept their place above the wreck by gravitational pull.
7. T F The octopus and the lobster were the predators of the Mary B.
8. T F The starfish is safe from enemies because of its spiny skin.
9. T F During winter months continuous darkness around the Mary B makes it impossible to know whether it is day or night.
10. T F The octopus has a beak which is shaped like that of a parrot.

Now check your answers with the key on page 114. Then determine your percentage of comprehension by checking in the table below.

Number of Answers Correct	10	9	8	7	6	5	4	3	2	1
Percentage of Comprehension	100	90	80	70	60	50	40	30	20	10

Reading Rate: In the spaces below fill in the times when you began and finished reading the selection. Subtract the beginning time from the ending time. Now check your rate of reading to the nearest time unit in the table below.

	Hour	Minutes	Seconds
Ending Time:	_____	_____	_____
Beginning Time:	_____	_____	_____
Total Reading Time:		_____	_____

Time	1'00"	1'15"	1'30"	1'45"	2'00"	2'15"	2'30"	2'45"
W.P.M.	810	650	540	460	405	360	320	295

Time	3'00"	3'15"	3'30"	3'45"	4'00"	4'15"	4'30"	4'45"
W.P.M.	270	250	230	215	200	190	180	170

LITERATURE POST-TEST

(679 words)

Purpose: To read as quickly as you can and still understand the general content of this selection.

Procedure: Record the time (hour, minutes, seconds) when you begin reading the selection. After reading the selection, again record the time. Then answer the questions related to the selection.

Beginning Time:

Hour: _____ Minutes: _____ Seconds: _____

Cortés Enters Cempoalla

As THEY approached the Indian city, they saw abundant signs of cultivation in the trim gardens and orchards that lined both sides of the road. They were now met by parties of the natives of either sex, who increased in numbers with every step of their progress. The women, as well as men,

William Prescott. From *The Oxford Anthology of American Literature*. Copyright 1938 by Oxford University Press, Inc. Pp. 676–7.

mingled fearlessly among the soldiers, bearing bunches and wreaths of flowers with which they decorated the neck of the general's charger, and hung a chaplet of roses about his helmet. Flowers were the delight of this people. They bestowed much care in their cultivation, in which they were well seconded by a climate of alternate heat and moisture, stimulating the soil to the spontaneous production of every form of vegetable life. The same refined taste, as we shall see, prevailed among the warlike Aztecs, and has survived the degradation of the nation in their descendants of the present day.

Many of the women appeared, from their richer dress and numerous attendants, to be persons of rank. They were clad in robes of fine cotton, curiously coloured, which reached from the neck—in the inferior orders, from the waist—to the ankles. The men wore a sort of mantle of the same material, à la Morisca, in the Moorish fashion, over their shoulders, and belts or sashes about the loins. Both sexes had jewels and ornaments of gold round their necks, while their ears and nostrils were perforated with rings of the same metal.

Just before reaching the town, some horsemen who had rode in advance returned with the amazing intelligence, "that they had been near enough to look within the gates, and found the houses all plated with burnished silver!" On entering the place, the silver was found to be nothing more than a brilliant coating of stucco, with which the principal buildings were covered; a circumstance which produced much merriment among the soldiers at the expense of their credulous comrades. Such ready credulity is a proof of the exalted state of their imaginations, which were prepared to see gold and silver in every object around them. The edifices of the better kind were of stone and lime, or bricks dried in the sun; the poorer were of clay and earth. All were thatched with palm-leaves, which, though a flimsy roof, apparently, for such structures, were so nicely interwoven as to form a very effectual protection against the weather.

The city was said to contain from twenty to thirty thousand inhabitants. This is the most moderate computation, and not improbable. Slowly and silently the little army paced the narrow and now crowded streets of Cempoalla, inspiring the natives with no greater wonder than they themselves experienced at the display of a policy and refinement so far superior to anything they had witnessed in the New World. The cacique came out in front of his residence to receive them. He was a tall and very corpulent man, and advanced leaning on two of his attendants. He received Cortés and his followers with great courtesy; and, after a brief interchange of civilities, assigned the army its quarters in a neighbouring temple, into the spacious courtyard of which a number of apartments opened, affording excellent accommodations for the soldiery.

Here the Spaniards were well supplied with provisions, meat cooked after the fashion of the country, and maize made into bread-cakes. The general received, also, a present of considerable value from the cacique, consisting of ornaments of gold and fine cottons. Notwithstanding these friendly demonstrations, Cortés did not relax his habitual vigilance, nor neglect any of the precautions of a good soldier. On his route, indeed, he had always marched in order of battle, well prepared against surprise. In his present quarters, he stationed his sentinels with like care, posted his small artillery so as to command the entrance, and forbade any soldier to leave the camp without orders, under pain of death.

Ending Time:

Hour: _____ Minutes: _____ Seconds: _____

LITERATURE II—*Cortés Enters Cempoalla*

Comprehension Check

Indicate whether, according to the selection just read, each of the following statements is true or false.

1. T F Flowers and vegetables grew very poorly in the hot climate of South America.
2. T F Indian women wore clothes of curiously colored cotton cloth.
3. T F Cortés found the Indians living in an uncivilized manner, having little time for enjoyment or beauty.
4. T F The houses of the Incas were covered with a thin coating of burnished silver.
5. T F The houses were made of stone, brick, or clay and were covered with a thatch of palm leaves.
6. T F Cortés was greeted in an unfriendly and discourteous manner by the Indians.
7. T F The Spaniards never relaxed their vigilance in dealing with the Indians.
8. T F It seemed that the Indians were vegetarians.
9. T F The Spaniards were allowed to enter the temple of the Indians.
10. T F It was found that the Indians lived mainly on cakes made from maize.

Now check your answers with the key on page 114. Then determine your percentage of comprehension by checking in the table below.

Number of Answers Correct	10	9	8	7	6	5	4	3	2	1
Percentage of Comprehension	100	90	80	70	60	50	40	30	20	10

Reading Rate: In the spaces below fill in the times when you began and finished reading the selection. Subtract the beginning time from the ending time. Now check your rate of reading to the nearest time unit in the table below.

	Hour	Minutes	Seconds
Ending Time:	_____	_____	_____
Beginning Time:	_____	_____	_____
Total Reading Time:		_____	_____

Time	1′00″	1′15″	1′30″	1′45″	2′00″	2′15″
W.P.M.	679	545	450	390	340	300

Time	2′30″	2′45″	3′00″	3′15″	3′30″	3′45″
W.P.M.	270	250	230	210	195	180

SCIENCE POST-TEST

Purpose: To read as quickly as you can and still understand the general content of this selection.

Procedure: Record the time (hour, minutes, seconds) when you begin reading the selection. After reading the selection, again record the time. Then answer the questions related to the selection.

Beginning Time:

Hour: _____ Minutes: _____ Seconds: _____

(850 words)

Chloroform

THE FIRST surgical operation to be carried out in Great Britain under ether vapour was at University College Hospital, London, and Sir R. Reynolds, who was present at it, writes of it as follows: "Liston had consented to try the anaesthetic: I can see him now as he said to his students: 'Gentlemen, we are now going to try a Yankee dodge for making men insensible.' . . . At length Peter Square said, 'He is ready now, sir.' Liston's knife flashed in the air: I took out my watch to count the time, and the leg was on the floor in six and twenty seconds. Liston turned to his students and said, 'This Yankee dodge, gentlemen, beats mesmerism.' " The curtness of the comment and the restraint of the report are thoroughly British.

The next scene in this story of the general anaesthetics is in Edinburgh and in the house of Dr. Simpson, a well-known Edinburgh gynaecologist. As a student, Simpson had watched Liston operate on a Highland woman without any anaesthetic and he had never forgotten what he had been forced to witness on that occasion. When therefore ether was introduced into England from America he immediately adopted it and used it in his obstetric practice. But he had not found ether entirely satisfactory in

Kenneth Walker. *The Story of Medicine.* Copyright 1954 by Kenneth Walker. Reprinted by permission of Oxford University Press. Pp. 212–14.

gynaecological work and he was now investigating other vapours that might possibly have anaesthetic properties. As his practice was a very large one the only time available for making trial of these vapours was usually at the end of a long day's work. The story of Simpson's discovery of the anaesthetic properties of chloroform has been told in a variety of ways, but the following accounts taken from a description given by Dr. Simpson's colleague, Professor Miller, is likely to be reliable. "Late one evening—it was the 4th of November 1847—on returning home after a weary day's work, Dr. Simpson, with his two friends and assistants, Drs. Keith and Duncan, sat down to their somewhat hazardous work in Dr. Simpson's dining-room. Having inhaled several substances, but without much effect, it occurred to Dr. Simpson to try a ponderous material which he had formerly set aside on a lumber table, and which on account of its great weight, he had hitherto regarded as of no likelihood whatever. That happened to be a small bottle of chloroform. It was searched for and recovered from beneath a heap of waste paper. And with each tumbler newly charged the inhalers resumed their vocation. Immediately an unwonted hilarity seized the party; they became bright-eyed, very happy and very loquacious—expatiating on the delicious aroma of the new fluid. The conversation was of unusual intelligence, and quite charmed the listeners—some ladies of the family and a naval officer, brother-in-law of Dr. Simpson.

"But suddenly there was a talk of sounds being heard like those of a cotton mill, louder and louder; a moment more and then all was quiet—and then crash. The inhaling party slipped off their chairs and flopped on the floor unconscious."

Professor Miller's report of the happenings of that night is a very full one and ends with a description of the experiences of each of the participants in the inhalation game as he or she "went under" and "came to." The lady previously mentioned as being one of the party, a niece of Mrs. Simpson, and in her report she states that she fell asleep quietly with her arms folded across her breast and in the very act of exclaiming: "I'm an angel. Oh I'm an angel." Everybody was delighted with the properties of the new vapour and Dr. Simpson himself was so satisfied that within a fortnight he had administered it to at least fifty of his patients. The results had been uniformly excellent.

Yet chloroform could not be introduced into medical practice in Scotland without provoking an outcry against it. Many people protested that its use in child-labour was contrary to all biblical teaching, for had not God said to Eve: "In sorrow thou shalt bring forth children"? Chloroform was, therefore, denounced from many a pulpit and in no uncertain terms. It was a "decoy of Satan," thundered one divine, "apparently offering itself to bless women; but in the end it will harden something and rob God of the deep and earnest cries which arise in time of trouble for help." Now, every Scot is something of a theologian and on hearing that his chloroform had been called a decoy of the Evil One, Simpson retorted that in the Holy Book could be found a full report of the first operation to be carried out under deep anaesthesia: "And the Lord God caused a deep sleep to fall upon Adam, and he slept; and He took one of his ribs and closed up the flesh instead thereof." This suggestion that God had created a precedent by making use of anaesthesia in His own work satisfied only a small section of the opposition and, as everybody knows, it was Queen Victoria who finally settled the ethics of the question of having chloroform administered to herself during the delivery of her seventh child, Prince Leopold. The announcement of this in the press was received with astonishment and grief, and even The Lancet was disturbed by it. The comment made by the Editor in May 1843 was as follows: "In no case could it be justifiable to administer chloroform in a perfectly ordinary labour." Yet the good Queen had allowed this and what the good Queen did was generally right. Again in 1857 the Queen accepted chloroform at her next confinement and thereafter chloroform became known in Great Britain as "anaesthesia à la Reine." The use of chloroform in childbirth was now considered fashionable and what was fashionable soon became moral.

Ending Time:

Hour: _____ Minutes: _____ Seconds: _____

SCIENCE II—*Chloroform*

Comprehension Check

Indicate whether, according to the selection just read, each of the following statements is true or false.

1. T F Dr. Simpson found ether particularly well suited to his gynaecological work.
2. T F The first surgical operation to be carried out in Great Britain under ether was performed by Dr. Liston.
3. T F Dr. Simpson is considered responsible for the discovery of the anaesthetic quality of chloroform.
4. T F The Scottish clergy hailed the introduction of chloroform to medical surgery as a great humanitarian advance.

5. T F To those who opposed him, Dr. Simpson defended his use of anaesthesia on precedent established in the Bible.

6. T F In general, the press of the middle 1800's was a staunch supporter of the use of anaesthesia.

7. T F The use of ether helped reduce the time required for many surgical operations.

8. T F Ether was introduced from England to America.

9. T F The chloroform first used by Dr. Simpson as an anaesthetic had a rather unpleasant odor.

10. T F Queen Victoria considered the use of chloroform as an anaesthetic to be immoral.

Now check your answers with the key on page 114. Then determine your percentage of comprehension by checking in the table below.

Number of Answers Correct	10	9	8	7	6	5	4	3	2	1
Percentage of Comprehension	100	90	80	70	60	50	40	30	20	10

Reading Rate: In the spaces below fill in the times when you began and finished reading the selection. Subtract the beginning time from the ending time. Now check your rate of reading to the nearest time unit in the table below.

	Hour	Minutes	Seconds
Ending Time:	_____	_____	_____
Beginning Time:	_____	_____	_____
Total Reading Time:	_____	_____	_____

Time	1'00"	1'15"	1'30"	1'45"	2'00"	2'15"	2'30"
W.P.M.	850	680	565	486	425	380	340

Time	2'45"	3'00"	3'15"	3'30"	3'45"	4'00"	4'15"	4'30"
W.P.M.	310	280	260	240	225	210	200	190

HISTORY POST-TEST

Purpose: To read as quickly as you can and still understand the general content of this selection.

Procedure: Record the time (hour, minutes, seconds) when you begin reading the selection. After reading the selection, again record the time. Then answer the questions related to the selection.

Beginning Time:

Hour: _____ Minutes: _____ Seconds: _____

(820 words)

The Oregon Trail

THE METHODS of the fur trade, and much of the personnel, were of French Canada. As in the Canada of Louis XIV, missionaries followed close on the heels of traders, but the missionaries in this instance were Protestant Yankees. In 1832 a group of Methodists under the Rev. Jason Lee joined a fur-trading party on the long overland route, and by 1834 had established a mission in the valley of the Willamette, which flowed into the Columbia at the site of Portland. Two years later a band of Presbyterians, including the energetic Dr. Marcus Whitman about whom a legend was soon built up, and the first white woman to cross the American continent, founded mission stations in the Walla Walla country, at the junction of the Snake and Columbia. Supply ships were sent to them round the Horn, and Dr. McLoughlin gave them every aid and encouragement, although he had more reason to favor the French Canadian priests who were coming to the Bitter Root valley and the Coeur d' Alene country, somewhat northward.

Proselytizing among the tribes of Oregon was not notably successful, but the missionaries in the Willamette valley found themselves in clover. Western Oregon has a de-lightfully mild and equable climate. The country was a mixture of open prairie with magnificent pine woods, rich soil for tillage, and natural meadows for grazing cattle. The missionaries' widely published letters spread the notion of Oregon as a home, while Washington Irving in his *Astoria* (1836) and *Adventures of Captain Bonneville* (1837) stressed the wilderness theme. Settlers began to arrive from New England; not many, to be sure, but enough to give Oregon a Yankee flavor.

In 1842 the "Oregon fever" struck the frontier folk of Iowa and Missouri, eager to renew their forest pioneering. Independence was the "jumping-off place" for the Oregon trail. Covered wagons converged there from the eastward in May, when the plains grass was fresh and green. More supplies were taken in, since hunting was a precarious source of food; and no help could be expected on the two-thousand-mile hike to the Willamette, unless from fur-trading posts that were not too well stocked themselves. Parties were organized, a captain appointed, an experienced trapper or fur trader engaged as pilot; and amid a great blowing of bugles and cracking of long whips, the caravan, perhaps a hundred wagons strong with thousands of cattle on the hoof, moved off up the west bank of the Missouri. At Fort Leavenworth, one of the bastions of the Indian frontier, the emigrants for the last time enjoyed the protection of their flag.

Near the Council Bluffs, where the Missouri is joined by the Platte, the Oregon trail turned west to follow the latter river over the Great Plains.* Until a road had been beaten into the sod, it was easy to lose the way. Numerous tributaries of the Platte, swollen and turbid in the spring of the year, had to be forded or swum, to the great damage of stores and baggage. Francis Parkman in 1846 found ancient tables and chests of drawers which perhaps had served some family in a dozen homes between England

Samuel Eliot Morison and Henry Steele Commager. *The Growth of the American Republic,* 4th ed. Copyright 1950 by Oxford University Press, Inc. Pp. 571–3.

---

* Later, the Oregon trail cut straight across the prairie from Independence to the southernmost bend of the Platte, near the site of Kearney, Nebraska.

and the Mississippi, left cracking in the sun where this latest wave of migration had grounded them. Every night the caravan made a hollow square of wagons round its fire of cottonwood or buffalo chips. Sentries stood guard to protect the hobbled horses and grazing cattle, and the howling of prairie wolves was drowned by the chorus of an old Appalachian ballad:

> Then o'er the hills in legions, boys,
> Fair freedom's star
> Points to the sunset regions, boys,
> Ha, ha! ha, ha!

Until the forks of the Platte were reached, near the present northeastern corner of Colorado, the herbage was luxuriant, and the grades easy. Following the north fork, the trail became hilly and then mountainous, as one turned north to avoid the Laramie spur of the Rockies. Beyond the South Pass came the worst part of the journey—a long, hard pull across the arid Wyoming basin, where the grass was scanty, and alkali deposits made the water almost undrinkable. Between the Gros Ventre and Teton ranges of the Rockies the Oregon emigrant found westward-flowing waters, and took heart; but there were still eight hundred miles to go to the lower Columbia, following the meanderings of the Snake river. As there was no good road in early days through the heavily forested country along the Columbia, wagons were often rafted down the stream; and with fair luck a party that left Independence in May might expect to celebrate Thanksgiving Day in the Willamette valley. But it was a lucky caravan indeed that arrived with the same number of souls that started; and some of the weaker parties disappeared—whether by starvation after losing the trail, or at the hands of Indians, no one knows.

Up to this time there had been no law in the Oregon country outside the Hudson's Bay settlement; and it speaks well for the character of the first emigrants that there was no crime. A group of Willamette valley settlers who gathered to hear a Fourth of July speech in 1843 remained to form a government by compact, as their ancestors had done in the Appalachian valleys. The heavy immigration of 1843–45, four to five thousand strong, including pioneers of lawless proclivities from Missouri, Arkansas, Iowa, and Illinois, strained the provisional organization, and convinced Congress that something must be done to provide this remote colony with government, law, and land titles. First, however, the Federal Government wished to reach a settlement with Great Britain.

Ending Time:

Hour: _____ Minutes: _____ Seconds: _____

HISTORY II—*The Oregon Trail*

Comprehension Check

Indicate whether, according to the selection just read, each of the following statements is true or false.

1. T F The Indians of Oregon embraced Christianity with eagerness.
2. T F The Oregon Trail became marked by the wagon tracks of the pioneers.
3. T F The early settlers in Oregon established a government, laws, and land titles.
4. T F The Oregon Trail wound through the present states of Missouri, Iowa, Nebraska, Colorado, and Wyoming.
5. T F The Oregon Territory was visited by Canadian fur traders and American missionaries.

6.   T F   The emigrants enjoyed little protection from Fort Leavenworth to the Willamette.
7.   T F   According to this account many people settled Oregon because they desired religious freedom.
8.   T F   Oregon was mainly settled by people from New England.
9.   T F   Most of the caravans were so well organized that few lives were lost.
10. T F   The Oregon Trail was almost three thousand miles in length.

Now check your answers with the key on page 114. Then determine your percentage of comprehension by checking in the table below.

Number of Answers Correct	10	9	8	7	6	5	4	3	2	1
Percentage of Comprehension	100	90	80	70	60	50	40	30	20	10

Reading Rate: In the spaces below fill in the times when you began and finished reading the selection. Subtract the beginning time from the ending time. Now check your rate of reading to the nearest time unit in the table below.

	Hour	Minutes	Seconds
Ending Time:	_____	_____	_____
Beginning Time:	_____	_____	_____
Total Reading Time:		_____	_____

Time	1′00″	1′15″	1′30″	1′45″	2′00″	2′15″	2′30″
W.P.M.	820	650	540	470	410	360	330

Time	2′45″	3′00″	3′15″	3′30″	3′45″	4′00″	4′15″
W.P.M.	300	270	250	230	220	205	190

PSYCHOLOGY POST-TEST

(869 words)

Purpose: To read as quickly as you can and still understand the general content of this selection.

Procedure: Record the time (hour, minutes, seconds) when you begin reading the selection. After reading the selection, again record the time. Then answer the questions related to the selection.

Beginning Time:

Hour: _____ Minutes: _____ Seconds: _____

Attitudes

AN ATTITUDE is a tendency toward uniformity of emotional response with respect to persons, objects, institutions, beliefs, or personal behavior; and expresses different degrees of acceptance or rejection. If one's feelings are for or against something his attitude possesses both direction and force. A child reflects an attitude in asserting that

Robert A. Davis. *Educational Psychology.* Copyright 1948 by McGraw-Hill Book Co., Inc. Pp. 109–12.

being honest in taking a test is important. He may support honesty in taking tests by refusing to accept opportunity to cheat. He may accept the principle simply as a moral precept which he has heard many times and yet occasionally cheat if he believes he may avoid detection.

The purposes of the school are significantly associated with children's attitudes. Classroom instruction varies in effectiveness according to the attitudes which children bring to school and those which such instruction creates in them. The value of subject matter may be considerably lessened, for example, if prejudice against science is inculcated in the child by home influences. Relationships with his teacher may be unsatisfactory if he manifests hostility as a result of conflicts with former teachers. Racial or religious bias may prevent his full co-operation with certain members of the class. He may possess implicit belief in all statements in textbooks, or he may be hypercritical of the truth of any statement read. He may have antisocial attitudes and accept cheating, "bluffing," and dishonesty as legitimate means of obtaining good school grades.

The teacher through his opportunity to direct instruction may cultivate attitudes that will free children's thinking from ignorance and prejudice. Although he may not without restraint dictate to them what they are to think, he may endeavor to aid them to learn how to think. He may teach them how to evaluate opinions critically and guide them in forming attitudes that encourage comprehensive treatment of reality.

HOW ATTITUDES ARE FORMED

One may have attitudes toward almost anything or anybody, although most attitudes are of low intensity until, through localization and discussion, they acquire strong positive or negative qualities. One may have fixed beliefs concerning the merits of an article of merchandise or toward the act of a friend. In this sense, attitudes may be considered specific. On the other hand, one may incorporate a broad personal ambition into a philosophy of life and maintain a consistent attitude toward the desirability of his purpose. Individuals may be conservative or liberal, and such a general attitude may surround many specific attitudes. One may be tolerant of gambling, believing that individuals should be allowed liberal bounds of personal freedom. Inconsistency between attitudes and behavior appears to occur more widely in general attitudes than in specific ones to the extent even of suggesting that the concept of a general attitude lacks validity.

Since attitudes are associated with emotions, they are generally unconsciously formed. Unlike interests, which seek immediate expression, attitudes may remain latent for long periods of time until opportunity for expression appears. Initially emotional products, they may be unexpressed in words until definite statements of opinion are demanded. Attitudes when so expressed may even then inadequately reflect true feelings. When an individual is asked for an opinion, his attitude is often revealed to himself for the first time. Intellectual processes may later be applied critically to an attitude, and it may become a reasoned conclusion. On the other hand, attitudes may be so highly emotionalized that one will reason illogically in order to preserve them.

Attitudes constitute the emotional residue of personal experiences and various items of information. If the reaction produces satisfaction or dissatisfaction, emotional learning occurs. Daily experiences provide the background for many of an individual's varied attitudes. Children, who in their English classes have read one book after another without developing interest or understanding, often generalize the effects of frustrated effort into an attitude that study of English literature is uninspiring. An unfavorable attitude already formed toward the school sometimes yields attitudes of narrower scope, such as the point of view that cheating in the classroom is justifiable. A single experience, if highly emotional, may have sufficient force to create an attitude. As a result of a single thoughtful act, a teacher may induce in a pupil a co-operative attitude; unjust punishment may result in a resentful one.

A particularly fertile source of attitudes is their acceptance in toto from other persons. Children overhear opinions expressed by parents and uncritically accept them as their own. Thus, white children who have few contacts with different races form racial attitudes on the basis of comments made by parents. Similarly they form unfavorable attitudes toward others on the basis of gossip.

The unconscious process through which attitudes are formed is a partial explanation of the frequent lack of logical foundation for an individual's attitudes. Since he is unaware that he is developing a point of view, he is unlikely to initiate effort toward its evaluation on the basis of adequate facts and logical reasoning. Not until an individual becomes aware that he possesses a definite attitude is there any likelihood that he may examine its logical basis. He may not know why he thinks as he does, for the experience that inspired his attitude long since may have been forgotten. Nor will he change his opinions and beliefs unless he has new experiences.

Ending Time:

Hour: _____ Minutes: _____ Seconds: _____

PSYCHOLOGY II—*Attitudes*

Comprehension Check

Indicate whether, according to the selection just read, each of the following statements is true or false.

1. T F An attitude expresses different degrees of acceptance or rejection.
2. T F Attitudes possess both direction and force.
3. T F An individual's learning in the classroom is directly affected by his attitudes.
4. T F Attitudes are generally formed unconsciously.
5. T F Attitudes generally reflect one's true feelings.
6. T F Attitudes develop independently of experiences.
7. T F Attitudes are generally closely associated with emotions.
8. T F Strong attitudes may cause an individual to reason illogically.
9. T F Attitudes are seldom passed directly from one individual to another.
10. T F If a person examines his attitudes logically it is usually possible for him to identify the experiences from which they originated.

Now check your answers with the key on page 114. Then determine your percentage of comprehension by checking in the table below.

Number of Answers Correct	10	9	8	7	6	5	4	3	2	1
Percentage of Comprehension	100	90	80	70	60	50	40	30	20	10

Reading Rate: In the spaces below fill in the times when you began and finished reading the selection. Subtract the beginning time from the ending time. Now check your rate of reading to the nearest time unit in the table below.

	Hour	Minutes	Seconds
Ending Time:	_____	_____	_____
Beginning Time:	_____	_____	_____
Total Reading Time:	_____		_____

Time	1′00″	1′15″	1′30″	1′45″	2′00″	2′15″	2′30″	2′45″
W.P.M.	871	697	580	497	435	388	349	318

Time	3′00″	3′15″	3′30″	3′45″	4′00″	4′15″	4′30″	4′45″	5′00″
W.P.M.	290	269	249	232	217	205	194	183	174

Comprehension Check Key

A. **NARRATIVE**—*The Mary B*

      1-T, 2-T, 3-F, 4-T, 5-T, 6-F, 7-T, 8-F, 9-F, 10-T

B. **LITERATURE**—*Cortés Enters Cempoalla*

      1-F, 2-T, 3-F, 4-F, 5-T, 6-F, 7-T, 8-F, 9-T, 10-F

C. **SCIENCE**—*Chloroform*

      1-F, 2-T, 3-T, 4-F, 5-T, 6-F, 7-T, 8-T, 9-F, 10-F

D. **HISTORY**—*The Oregon Trail*

      1-F, 2-T, 3-F, 4-F, 5-T, 6-T, 7-F, 8-F, 9-F, 10-F

E. **PSYCHOLOGY**—*Attitudes*

      1-T, 2-T, 3-T, 4-T, 5-F, 6-F, 7-T, 8-T, 9-F, 10-T

Summary of Flexibility Tests

AFTER HAVING read the five selections in the Flexibility Post-Test, enter the indicated information for each selection in the table below. Complete the table by transferring to it the information from the table containing the Flexibility Pre-Test results on page 17.

Kind of Material	PRE- and POST-FLEXIBILITY TEST SUMMARY				
	Test	Selection	Rate (W.P.M.)	Comprehension Percentage
Narrative	Pre-	Rest Stop for the Sanderlings		
	Post-	The Mary B		
Literature	Pre-	Cortés Makes an Ally		
	Post-	Cortés Enters Cempoalla		
Science	Pre-	Development of Anaesthesia		
	Post-	Chloroform		
History	Pre-	Washington, Farmer-President		
	Post-	The Oregon Trail		
Psychology	Pre-	Interests		
	Post-	Attitudes		

You now have the information necessary to compare your performance on the two tests of reading flexibility. To do this two steps are necessary:

1. On the graph on page 18 enter the reading rates attained on each of the five selections in the Flexibility Post-Test. This will permit you to compare your own figures from each selection in the two flexibility tests.

Does the line connecting the rates obtained on the Flexibility Post-Test more closely resemble line "A" than did the line connecting the rates from the Flexibility Pre-Test?

2. Insert the figures called for in the following spaces:

Flexibility Pre-Test	Highest Rate	_____
	Lowest Rate	_____
	Range of Reading Rate	_____
Flexibility Post-Test	Highest Rate	_____
	Lowest Rate	_____
	Range of Reading Rate	_____

Post-Test Range of Rate	_____
Pre-Test Range of Rate	_____
Change in Range of Rate	_____

Determine your increase in Range of Reading Rate (Flexibility) by subtracting the Pre-Test Range of Reading Rate from the Post-Test Range of Reading Rate. If you have become a more flexible reader during the past few weeks you will note two differences between the results of the Flexibility Pre-Test and Post-Test.

1. The rate at which you read material has increased. Both your highest and lowest reading rates on the Post-Test selections exceed the highest and lowest reading rates on the Pre-Test selections.

2. The range between the highest and lowest reading rates on the Post-Test selection exceeds the range between the highest and lowest reading rates on the Pre-Test selections. In other words, your range of reading rate has increased. You have become a more flexible reader.

VOCABULARY POST-TEST

Roots of Words

How WELL do you know the important roots of English words? Below are listed ten Latin and ten Greek roots which are the base for many English words. Write a meaning for each root and list at least two words that are derived from each root.

Latin root	*Meaning*	*English words*
1. plico		
2. specio		
3. teneo		
4. multus		
5. capio		
6. ego		
7. ignis		
8. locus		
9. pes, pedis		
10. pater		

Greek root	*Meaning*	*English words*
1. bios		
2. chromos		
3. heteros		
4. orthos		
5. pan		
6. poly		
7. psyche		
8. tele		
9. micro		
10. grapho		

Prefixes

Do you know the meaning of the following prefixes? Write what each prefix means to you and then write two words in which the prefix appears.

Prefix	Meaning	Words
1. de		
2. per		
3. un		
4. ex		
5. pre		
6. inter		
7. non		
8. com		
9. ac		
10. be		

Suffixes

Do you know the meaning of the following suffixes? Write what each suffix means to you and then write two words in which the suffix appears.

Suffix	Meaning	Words
1. ance		
2. er		
3. ist		
4. ful		
5. ible		
6. less		
7. ment		
8. ion		
9. ory		
10. ous		

Antonyms

WORDS that have a meaning opposite to other words are called antonyms. In each of the rows below, you will find *one* word that means the opposite of the key word. Underline this word or antonym.

Key Word

1. belittle   deprecate   minimize   depreciate   aggrandize
2. abhorrent   detestable   admirable   hateful   abominable
3. furtive   stealthy   forthright   surreptitious   covert
4. partisan   follower   disciple   adversary   adherent
5. cadaverous   stout   pinched   gaunt   worn

Key Word

6. imply   involve comprehend express implicate
7. deleterious   detrimental noxious salutatory baneful
8. pompous   lowly showy ostentatious pretentious
9. exasperate   provoke mollify nettle roil
10. redundant   wordy concise diffuse verbose

Synonyms

OUR language is rich in descriptive words. Words that mean the same or about the same as other words are called synonyms.

In each row of words below you will find three that are synonyms of the key word and one that is not. Underline in each row the synonyms of the key word.

Key Word

1. lassitude   lethargy languor vigor torpidity
2. facetious   jocose lugubrious witty humorous
3. diligent   sedulous dilatory assiduous busy
4. catholic   universal cosmic parochial cosmopolitan
5. bully   cow bulldoze cajole intimidate
6. recoil   confront shrink blench quail
7. adamant   obdurate inexorable inflexible yielding
8. saturnine   dour genial sullen glum
9. artless   ingenuous affected natural naïve
10. oblique   crooked askew devious ironic

KEY TO VOCABULARY POST-TEST

Roots of Words

SEVERAL words are listed under English words for each group. The student may list other words than these, however. The words they list should be checked for accuracy in the dictionary.

Latin root	Meaning	English words
1. plico	fold	appliance, comply
2. specio	see, observe	inspect, respect
3. teneo	hold, have	tenant, tenure
4. multus	many, much	multitude, multiply
5. capio	seize, take	decapitate, capture
6. ego	I, myself	egoist, egoism
7. ignis	fire	ignite, ignition
8. locus	place	locate, location
9. pes, pedis	foot	centipede, pedestal
10. pater	father	paternal, paternity

Greek root	Meaning	English words
1. bios	life	biography, biology
2. chromos	time	chronology, chronograph
3. heteros	other	heterodox, heterogeneous
4. orthos	correct	orthodox, orthodontist
5. pan	all, whole	pan-American, pantheism
6. poly	much, many	polygamy, polysyllabic
7. psyche	soul, mind	psychic, psychology
8. tele	far off	telephone, telegraph
9. micro	small	microscope, micrometer
10. grapho	to write	graphic, monograph

Prefixes

UNDER the column headed Words, a few words containing the prefix are given. There are many others, of course, and if the student lists them they should be checked in the dictionary.

Prefix	Meaning	Words
1. de	down, away	descent, depart
2. per	through, by	perceive, perforate
3. un	not	unknown, unable
4. ex	formerly, out	exhale, ex-convict
5. pre	before	prelude, preamble
6. inter	among, between	international, intercede
7. non	not	non-committal, nondescript
8. com	with, together	commend, compact
9. ac	to, toward	acquire, acclimate
10. be	about, over	bedim, bedew

Suffixes

UNDER the column headed Words, a few words containing the suffix are given. There are many others, of course, and if the student lists them they should be checked in the dictionary.

Suffix	Meaning	Words
1. ance	action, process	assistance, abundance
2. er	one who, process of	teacher, dinner
3. ist	one who practices a given action	pianist, scientist
4. ful	full of, characterized by	hopeful, beautiful
5. ible	having quality of fitness	credible, digestible
6. less	without, beyond the range of	tasteless, pointless
7. ment	state, condition, quality	discouragement, amazement
8. ion	act of, state of	oppression, confession
9. ory	place of, that which pertains to	rectory, offertory
10. ous	full of, having qualities of	joyous, harmonious

Antonyms

THE antonym to the key word is underlined.

Key Word

1. belittle	deprecate minimize depreciate aggrandize
2. abhorrent	detestable admirable hateful abominable
3. furtive	stealthy forthright surreptitious covert
4. partisan	follower disciple adversary adherent
5. cadaverous	stout pinched gaunt worn
6. imply	involve comprehend express implicate
7. deleterious	detrimental noxious salutatory baneful
8. pompous	lowly showy ostentatious pretentious
9. exasperate	provoke mollify nettle roil
10. redundant	wordy concise diffuse verbose

Synonyms

THE synonyms of the key word are underlined.

Key Word

1. lassitude	lethargy languor vigor torpidity
2. facetious	jocose lugubrious witty humorous
3. diligent	sedulous dilatory assiduous busy
4. catholic	universal cosmic parochial cosmopolitan
5. bully	cow bulldoze cajole intimidate
6. recoil	confront shrink blench quail
7. adamant	obdurate inexorable inflexible yielding
8. saturnine	dour genial sullen glum
9. artless	ingenuous affected natural naïve
10. oblique	crooked askew devious ironic